Thirukkural

A Snapshot of the Sastras?

Kathiravan Krishnamurthi, Ph.D.,

BOOK DETAILS

Title	Thirukkural
	A Snapshot of the Sastras?
Author's Name	Kathiravan Krishnamurthi
Pages	190
Published by	MIN E KAVI (மின்கவி)
Publisher details	MIN E KAVI (மின்கவி) (E-Development & Digital Publishing) www.minekavi.com Phone: 9626227537
Edition	I
ISBN	978-93-94743-85-4
Copyrights:	© Author

CONTENTS

Foreword   I
Preface   XI
Introduction   1
Chapter 1   Aram: The Universal Path   5
Chapter 2   The Difference between Aram and Dharma   13
Chapter 3   Rain: Worship, Charity, and Penance   27
Chapter 4   Learning, Education, and Knowledge   36
Chapter 5   Hospitality: The Householder's Lofty Virtue   44
Chapter 6   The Exemplar: Valluvar's Model Citizen   50
Chapter 7   Anthanars and Brahmins: Are they
              Different?   54
Chapter 8   The Light of Truth that Guides Exemplars   65
Chapter 9   The Ideal Country: Safety, Wealth, the
              Leader, and the People   72
Chapter 10   How Competent People Act   79
Chapter 11   Model Citizen's Duty to Society   90
Chapter 12   Ethical Wealth Acquisition   98
Chapter 13   The Life of a Householder on the Path of
              Aram   110
Chapter 14   Humility and Self-Restraint: The Passports
              to Immortality   119
Chapter 15   Excellence of Wife and Children   128
Chapter 16   How to Use Word Power Successfully   131
Chapter 17   Nagaswamy's Other Acts of Commission
              and Omission   139
Conclusions   149
Appendix: Coupling of Kurals   151
References   162

Foreword

Thirukkural was written by Thiruvalluvar (also referred to as Valluvar) about 2,000 years ago. At the time he wrote his masterpiece, Aryans had already infiltrated Tamil Nadu and were actively promoting their philosophy and their religion. Their religion was the Vedic religion based on the Vedas and Upanishads. Their laws, customs, and norms were based on Manusmriti. Their philosophy and their customs were completely different from the prevailing philosophical ideas and the way of life of the Tamils.

For several reasons, Thirukkural attracted very little attention from scholars and the public during the following several centuries. Also, due to the Aryan influence, Hinduism became the dominant religion of Tamil Nadu and the rest of India. During the 11th century CE, the book called Thiruvalluvamaalai, an anthology of short poems by fifty-five poets, appeared on the Tamil literary scene to promote Thirukkural and elevate it to its rightful place, after which Thirukkural received wider publicity. Manakkudavar, a Jain scholar, wrote a detailed commentary on Thirukkural and viewed it as secular literature. Following Manakkudavar, a few more scholars wrote commentaries on Thirukkural.

I

During the 14th century, the famous Brahmin commentator Parimelazhagar wrote a detailed commentary in which he interpreted the secular treatise Thirukkural strictly from the Aryan standpoint.

Parimelazhagar was not alone in interpreting Thirukkural from the point of view of Hinduism. Whenever Thirukkural became prominent and popular, many Brahmin scholars twisted Thiruvalluvar's ideas and tried to assert that they were nothing but a synopsis of the Aryan Sastras. After Thirukkural appeared in print format in 1812, many scholars worldwide took note of its grandeur and expressed their admiration and appreciation for Thiruvalluvar's wisdom and its universal applicability. During the second half of the 20th century, Thirukkural became an integral part of the school curriculum in Tamil Nadu. More translations of Thirukkural appeared in several languages of the world. In the past twenty years, Thirukkural has even been quoted by cabinet ministers in Indian parliamentary discussions. Irritated by the increasing popularity of Thirukkural, Hindu religious zealots once again started to question the originality of Thirukkural. They began a propaganda campaign, claiming that Thirukkural is really based on other religious texts; they also expressed doubts about its authenticity. Nagaswamy's book, *Thirukural – An Abridgement of Sastras*, is the latest attempt to misinterpret Thirukkural and claim that it is nothing but a summary of the Hindu Sastras. In this book, the author, Dr. Kathiravan Krishnamurthi, systematically exposes Nagaswamy's mischievous attempt to deliberately distort the truth to suit his illogical conclusion that Thirukkural is an abridgment of the Sastras. Dr. Kathiravan Krishnamurthi's book, *Thirukkural: A Snapshot of the Sastras?* offers a fitting rebuttal to Nagaswamy's book.

The foundation of the Vedic religion is Varnashrama dharma, which says that the [1]Lord created four classes of people: the Brahmin, the Kshatriya, the Vaisya, and the Sudra, from his mouth, arms, thighs, and feet, respectively. Of these four classes, the Brahmins were considered the most superior class. The next three classes are the Kshatriyas, Vaisyas, and Sudras. Each class of people has pre-determined duties. The Brahmins are priests, the Kshatriyas warriors, and the Vaisyas businesspeople and agriculturists. The only duty assigned to the Sudras was to serve the other three higher classes.

(1 Manusmriti 1:31, Bhagavad – Gita 4:13)

In contrast to the Aryans, the Tamils considered that all people were equal, and they did not subscribe to the Aryan idea of stratifying society into four classes. The author, Dr. Kathiravan Krishnamurthi, cites Kurals 972 and 973, pointing out that Thiruvalluvar categorically states that all are equal by birth and that one's high or low status is only determined by one's conduct and not by one's birth. The author poses the following logical question: If Thirukkural is incompatible with the foundation of the Vedic religion, how can it be considered an abridgment of the Sastras? Further, it should be noted that Nagaswamy conveniently ignores any reference to Kurals 972 and 973 in his book.

The other aspect of Varnashrama dharma is the four stages of life. The Vedic religion advocates the social doctrine of the four stages of life. It maintains that one should first become a celibate student; then become a married householder, discharging his duties to his ancestors by begetting sons and his duties to the gods by conducting sacrifices; then retire with or without his wife to the forest to devote himself to spiritual contemplation; and finally, become a homeless wandering ascetic and devote himself to the pursuit of liberation (salvation). Tamil society did not have these four stages of life. Although there were a few ascetics, the lifestyle of a householder was considered superior to that of an ascetic. Dr. Kathiravan Krishnamurthi points out several relevant kurals where Valluvar emphasizes that the householder's way of life is superior to that of the ascetic.

Nagaswamy does not produce any evidence from the Sastras supporting the idea that the domestic lifestyle is superior to the ascetic lifestyle. If there is no concordance between Thirukkural and the Sastras on this critical topic, how can Thirukkural be considered an abridgment of the Sastras?

In this book, Dr. Kathiravan Krishnamurthi points out several instances where facts do not support Nagaswamy's claim that Thirukkural is an abridgment of the Sastras. For example, in Chapter 4, the author compares the profound ideas in chapter 39 of Thirukkural on learning and education with the one irrelevant passage quoted by Nagaswamy from Arthasastra, and points out that it is clearly insufficient on this basis to conclude that this chapter of Thirukkural has been abridged from the Sastras.

In Chapter 5, Dr. Kathiravan Krishnamurthi observes that whereas Valluvar states that guests should be served the best food by the host irrespective of who they are, the quote from Dharmasastra mentions that the host should eat only after feeding the gods, sages, guests, manes, and household deities. The quoted passage includes a whole list of who should be served. This passage has no relevance to Valluvar's ideas on hospitality. This is another example where Nagaswamy appears to compare apples to oranges.

In Chapter 6, the author cites yet another example where the facts do not support Nagaswamy's thesis. In Kural 69, Valluvar says that a mother rejoices even more than at the birth of her son when she hears that her son is a perfect gentleman with every desirable quality (an exemplar). Nagaswamy says that this statement of Valluvar is an echo from the Sastras and quotes the following passage: "If the son upholds by his intellect, virtues, strength, and the name of the family, then only the mother truly attains motherhood." This quote from the Sastras has no relevance to Kural 69. Therefore, the author rightly says that the conclusion that Kural 69 echoes the above passage from the Sastras is nothing but a figment of Nagaswamy's imagination.

In Chapter 7, the author convincingly proves that the term "Anthanar" in Thirukkural is not equivalent to the term "Brahmin," as Nagaswamy and Sanskrit scholars claim. In

Chapter 8, the author provides another example of Nagaswamy's failure to justify his conclusions. In Kural 299, Valluvar mentions that truth is the guiding light for an exemplar. Here again, Nagaswamy quotes an irrelevant passage from the Sastras to conclude that Kural 299 has the same idea as the Sastras. In Chapter 9, the author describes Valluvar's concept of an ideal country in detail and notes that Nagaswamy fails to provide any passage from the Sastras to match Valluvar's profound ideas about countries. In the subsequent chapters—10 through 17—the author clearly rebuts Nagaswamy's unsuccessful attempts to justify his claim that Thirukkural is an abridgment of the Sastras.

One can always find isolated examples of similarities between different works by different authors. For example, there is a lot of similarity between the Analects of Confucius and Thirukkural. We can also find some commonalities between The Ten Commandments and Thirukkural. There is considerable similarity between the Bible and Thirukkural. Based on these accidental similarities, one should not come to the hasty conclusion that one is an abridgment of the other. Nagaswamy's attempt to convince the reader that Thirukkural is an abridgment of the Sastras is an example of a Hindu zealot's overenthusiastic myopia.

It is a deliberate attempt on his part to malign Thirukkural and to insult the intelligence of famous scholars such as Albert Schweitzer, Rabindranath Tagore, Kamil Zvelebil, et al., who have expressed their unqualified admiration for Thirukkural as a secular text.

Dr. Kathiravan Krishnamurthi's book clearly shows his in-depth knowledge of Thirukkural and the Sastras. This book undoubtedly presents a convincing argument why Nagaswamy's book, *Thirukural – An Abridgement of Sastras*, must be rejected as an ill-conceived attempt to belittle the greatness of Valluvar's magnum opus, Thirukkural, which serves as a guiding light to humanity.

I congratulate Dr. Kathiravan Krishnamurthi for drafting this excellent book, and I appreciate his efforts for digging deep into Thirukkural and the Sastras to write this much-needed criticism of the unsubstantiated claim by Nagaswamy that Thirukkural is an abridgment of the Sastras. This book is a must-read for all those who have not read Nagaswamy's book, because it will help them understand the real relationship between Thirukkural and the Sastras. More importantly, this book must definitely be read by everyone who has already read Nagaswamy's book, so that they can understand the real truth about Thirukkural and realize that it is *not* an abridgment of the Sastras.

Dr. R. Prabhakaran

Bel Air (Retd.)

Maryland

United States

x

Preface

Thirukkural is a Tamil literary work on the art of living. It has been widely translated into more than forty languages. It addresses people of all ethnicities, castes, races, religions, and countries of origin. In the ancient Indian context, Thirukkural first differentiated itself by treating people of all castes equally. Written about two thousand years ago, its profundity still makes it an interesting topic of study across many countries and people. The book is divided into three sections – Aram (Virtue), Porul (Wealth), and Inbam (Eros) – with 133 chapters and 10 maxims per chapter. The work thus comprises 1,330 maxims.

However, there always has been a strong tendency to view the content of the section on Virtue historically through the framework of the Dharmasastra texts, especially Manusmriti; the section on Wealth through Kautilya's Arthasastra; and the section on Eros through Vatsyayana's Kamasutra. There are some scholars who assume that Thirukkural is indebted to these prior Sanskrit texts. Some of them even argue that Thirukkural borrowed heavily from

Sanskrit literature while adapting its content in distinctively Tamil ways.

Although this approach remained largely confined to restricted circles with small essays on selective topics, a book appeared recently that claims the entire Thirukkural is an abridgment of the Sastras. The author supports his claims by interpreting Thirukkural selectively. He also gives quotations from the Sastras that he claims are parallel to Thirukkural. The author, Nagaswamy, makes many tall claims in his book; for example, he claims to have "proved" that Thirukkural is a derivative book of the Hindu Vedic tradition. He further goes on to claim that Valluvar based his text on the four-varna (caste) system of the Vedic faith.

Tamil scholars who have studied Thirukkural in depth have responded with rebuttals; Manjai Vasanthan, in particular, authored a book in Tamil explaining the fallacies of Nagaswamy's thesis. The idea of my book stems from a critical perspective of Thirukkural study and interpretation. I have studied Nagaswamy. I have also studied many commentaries on Thirukkural, which inspired me to write a critique of Nagaswamy's conclusion.

I have carefully chosen a few important topics and examined them in detail to show that Thirukkural's ideas are fundamentally different from those of the Sastras. First, we develop a counter-hypothesis to Nagaswamy's hypothesis and proceed to show that Thirukkural's ethos is antithetical to that of the Sastras. We learn how Thirukkural is organized and how it needs careful and honest study. We try to make it easy for the reader to discern the fundamental differences between Thirukkural's ideas, philosophy, and ethos and those of the Sastras. In the process, we have provided examples of how the maxims are arranged in the chapters, how each maxim is positioned within each chapter and referenced in other chapters, and how all of these interlinkages must be understood to absorb the complete message of the text. In the examples, we show how contextual study and complete understanding of the interlinkages will lead the reader to see the irreconcilable differences between the messages conveyed by Thirukkural and the Sastras.

We invite the reader on an invigorating journey. To facilitate reading, each chapter is self-contained and has its own conclusion. We have tried to present a methodical approach to understanding Thirukkural and appreciating how its message differs from those of Sanskrit works. We have shared firsthand experiences with Thirukkural in real life situations. We have also spotlighted the relevance of Thirukkural's wisdom to many of the issues and challenges we face today.

Finally, I am indebted to my friends – Annamalai Prabhakar, Gurusamy Manivannan, and Sethu Subbar – who took the time to read the draft, suggest improvements, and point out errors. The book was copyedited by my college friend and copy editor par excellence, Santhosh Matthew Paul. I dedicate this work to all young readers who are not afraid to raise critical questions in their quest for the truth.

Introduction

"One should never contemplate the couplets in isolation. We must again and again stress that they have true validity and meaning only in their patterned relation to other couplets, and to the whole. And when read and contemplated in this way, Thiruvalluvar's ethics is never that of a Chanakya or a Machiavelli." K. Zvelebil

"The Bhagavad Gita and Thirukkural tell us to do our duty and expect no reward," said one of my friends enthusiastically, as though he had discovered something new. I was momentarily shocked, then recovered my wits. I asked him, "Are you sure Valluvar said that in Thirukkural?" He was certain and quoted the maxim from Thirukkural. He went on to tell me that Valluvar's message is the same as Lord Krishna's. I narrated a short story to explain the context of Valluvar's maxim, the chapter it was presented in, and the message itself, deciphering it from the original text in Tamil.

First, Valluvar does not use an imperative or sermonizing tone in Thirukkural. His message is usually conveyed in an indirect and allusive fashion. Second, when we situate the maxim that my friend quoted in its chapter and look at the context, it becomes clear that Valluvar is talking about exemplary human beings who sense the needs of the people around them and help them out of selfless benevolence, without expecting anything in return. In this maxim, Valluvar describes an ideal member of society, a role model, an exemplar. He ascribes many lofty qualities to this exemplar. A chapter is devoted to one of these qualities (selfless benevolence), and my friend was quoting a maxim from this chapter. This is not the same as the wartime sermon given by Krishna to Arjuna: "Do your duty; expect no reward."

Thirukkural is an original classic masterpiece on the art of living. It is written in Tamil and has been translated into many languages. The work encompasses many aspects of living that are relevant even today. Thirukkural is divided into three cantos: Virtue, Wealth, and Pleasure. The author, Valluvar, composed his aphorisms in poetic form. "Valluvar addresses the whole community of humankind, irrespective of caste, ethnicity, or belief, in the language of sovereign morality and absolute reason" (M. Ariel in Pope [1886]).

We are living in the age of information and social media. Many authors with their own personal agenda are vying for our attention, their ulterior goal being to drive us in a certain direction. Their views are aligned with a narrative that is foisted on an unsuspecting public by a well-oiled propaganda machine. In recent times, there is an increasing focus in certain circles on claiming that most literary works in India were drawn from Sanskrit Sastras and Smritis. Instead of appreciating the diversity and heterogeneity of many of these works, there is a motivated attempt to homogenize them. More specifically, even divergent ideas are appropriated and misrepresented as having originated from one dominant source or fountain. There is a disturbing trend of not reading, listening to, and appreciating value systems that are completely different from the dominant narrative.

One such attempt that attracted wide coverage and publicity is *Thirukural: An Abridgement of Sastras* by R. Nagaswamy. The author claims to have studied Thirukkural from a new, revolutionary perspective. The claim that "citing extensively from Sanskrit works such as Manu's Dharmasastra, Kautilya's Arthasastra, and Vatsayana's Kamasutra, we prove Thirukkural is a derivative book of [the] Hindu Vedic tradition" elicited a response from Tamil scholars and thinkers.

Is Thirukkural indeed a derivative book of the Hindu Vedic tradition? If so, how? If not, why not?

As engineers, scientists, and sociologists trained to solve real-world problems, we can use methods known to us to deal with the question of whether Thirukkural is an abridgment of the Sastras. These methods are applied to information drawn from textbooks, commentaries, translations, and other resources. Based on this research, we can develop our own set of hypotheses for studying Valluvar and Sastras, analyze texts by carefully examining the evidence, interpret and publish the results. This book is the result of such an effort.

Chapter 1

Aram: The Universal Path

Aram is a special word that indicates good deeds. It is formed from two words: aRu (அறு) and am (அம்). The first word means "cut through." Aram is used to cut away obstacles and clear the path ahead. As we travel through life, it presents us with many problems. Aram helps us deal with these hurdles. Aram is a collection of disciplined methods devised by the wise to help its practitioners lead a fulfilling life. Over time, Aram expanded to a powerful word conveying rich connotations such as goodness, charity, and even justice. Aram encompasses the many good qualities needed to lead a successful and happy life. In general, Aram embodies virtues and the associated good deeds.

Thoughts are the basis of orderly conduct and discipline. Pure thoughts lead to good and kind words, leading to good actions (deeds). Thoughts are static; words and actions are the dynamic counterparts of thought. For thoughts to be pure, the mind should be free of blemishes; actions will then follow the righteous path of Aram. Valluvar lays down a philosophical definition of Aram in maxims 34 and 35:

மனத்துக்கண் மாசிலன் ஆதல் அனைத்தறன்
ஆகுல நீர பிற (34)

Right action is purity of mind – everything else is fruitless.

He says, "The spotless mind is the fountain of righteousness; everything else is just vanity." He further goes on to define the "spotless mind" in maxim 35:

அழுக்காறு அவாவெகுளி இன்னாச்சொல்
நான்கும்
இழுக்கா இயன்றது அறம் (35)

Envy, desire, anger, bitter words – virtue
is devoid of all four.

Maxim 35 deals with the absence of the following bad qualities: envy, desire anger, and the use of bitter words. Whereas maxim 34 talks about the attributes of an unpolluted mind, maxim 35 deals with the pollutants, that is, the habits and qualities that make a person deviate from the path of Aram. Thus, maxim 34 defines Aram in terms of its attributes, whereas maxim 35 lists some flaws that have to be negated before one can achieve the ideal: a spotless mind. Many commentators have looked at maxims 34 and 35 as a pair: the first talks about a spotless mind, and the second suggests a possible way to achieve it.

As we proceed to read Valluvar, we find that he implicitly draws a picture of righteousness that would bring long-lasting wealth and fame for the adherent; the deviant could experience a downfall. A faultless mind without greed, jealousy, anger, and the use of hurtful words constitutes the strong basis of his Aram. Aram is freely adopted as a goal-oriented ethic by a person who has firm convictions about its utility; it is followed by one who is liberated, and its practice brings boundless joy. Valluvar's virtues are thus based on the ideals he envisages and will lead an individual to experience enduring joy in his or her life.

Aram, the Universal Principle

Valluvar's Aram is not just the primary section of his work, but the core overarching principle that underlies it. This is the feature of his book that distinguishes it from Sanskrit works on wealth, pleasure, and the art of living. Valluvar's Aram is the underlying fiber drawing together all the other strands that he weaves. Aram underpins the body of his work, whether the topic is family life, running a business or kingdom, or experiencing pleasure. This universality of Aram refutes the claims made by Nagaswamy in his book *Thirukural: An Abridgement of Sastras* that Thirukkural is an abridgment of the Sastras.

This overarching concept of Aram is implicit in most of Valluvar's work. The careful reader of Thirukkural will recognize this element as she reads the entire book. However, Valluvar does state this concept explicitly in a few places, for example, in maxim 39:

அறத்தான் வருவதே இன்பம் மற்றெல்லாம்
புறத்த புகழும் இல   (39)

Right action brings happiness – the rest
earn no fame.

Aram guides everything that matters in life. Aram is also emphasized in government and business matters, which fall outside the realm of family life. True fame and joy in this world are earned by leading a virtuous life.

Nagaswamy, without understanding this universality of Aram, has erred by linking various unconnected sources to Valluvar's work. The disparate works that he cites to fit his "abridgment thesis" do not resonate with our thesis.

Manu's Dharmasastra, Kautilya's Arthasastra, and Vatsayana's Kamasutra do not have this overarching emphasis on virtue. In our thesis, we will take many couplets, analyze them, and see for ourselves how they convey an essence that is different from that of Sanskrit works. In doing this, we are educating ourselves and our readers in order to clear up the misunderstanding created by Nagaswamy's book.

If Thirukkural is merely an abridgment of a large body of work (Sastras), the essence of the Sastras must be present in Thirukkural. The various Sastras that are brought to support the claim of abridgment—Dharmasastra and Arthasastra—taken together do not have anything in common with the sentiments expressed in Valluvar's work. Though Valluvar's treatise has sections on Aram (virtue), Porul (wealth), and Inbam (Love and Joy), a common overarching ethos permeates the entire text; virtue supersedes gathering wealth and seeking pleasure. This conclusion is based on a reading of the entire text, but Valluvar is emphatic in the second section (on wealth):

Wealth acquired legitimately without harming anybody will bring joy and facilitate virtue.

அறனீனும் இன்பமும் ஈனும் திறன்அறிந்து
தீதின்றி வந்த பொருள் (பொருள்-754)

Wealth gained without harm grants
both virtue and joy.

Valluvar passionately advocates the virtue of giving and sharing. He says, "Having plenty and reserving all of it for oneself is more miserable than begging (Virtue – 229)." This is his unequivocal advice to all, irrespective of caste or creed. He would love humans to imitate the crow, which invites all of its kind to share what it has found without hiding it (527).

இரத்தலின் இன்னாது மன்ற நிரப்பிய
தாமே தமியர் உணல் (229)

More bitter than begging – is filling up coffers
and eating alone.

காக்கை கரவா கரைந்துண்ணும் ஆக்கமும்
அன்னநீ ரார்க்கே உள (பொருள் - 527)

Crows, without concealing their food, caw and eat
together – for those like them assets grow.

However, Manu, who advocates the division of society on
the basis of birth, says, "A brahmana shall not offer advice
to a Sudra, nor the leavings, nor what has been prepared as
an offering to the Gods. He shall not expound the law to
him; nor shall he indicate to him any penance" — (4.80)

Thirukkural is unique in weaving the ethos of virtue (Aram)
into the gathering of wealth (Porul). The ideas of the
sections are tightly coupled. Nagaswamy, in his entire work,
has not quoted a single analogue in the Sastras for this
emphasis on universal virtue that applies to all, irrespective
of their caste or station in life.

Chapter 2

The Difference between Aram and Dharma

Dharma as described by the Sastras is vastly different from the Aram propounded by Thiruvalluvar. Manu divided human society into four birth-based castes (Brahmanas, Kshatriyas, Vaishyas, and Sudras), described laws governed by caste, and defined Dharma. In India, this traditionally included one's duty by virtue of being part of a particular stratum of society, a caste (*varna*) or birth group (*jati*). In Rig Veda X.90, a creation hymn, the four broad *varnas* emerge from the parts of the body of the divine being who created the universe. From his head arose the priests and scholars (Brahmins); from his arms, the kings, and warriors (Kshatriyas); from his thighs, the farmers and merchants (Vaishyas); and from his feet, the servants and laborers (Sudras). The hierarchy and stratification of society is thus embedded in the blueprint of the universe. At the same time, the interdependence of the castes is recognized, for they are parts of one body, one organism.

Dharma is not the same for each of these castes. Duty, vocation, and even moral obligations are different for the Brahmin priest and for the king. Dharma differs for women and for men, for young persons and for elders. "Better one's own Dharma, though imperfect, than another's Dharma well performed," says Krishna in the Bhagavad Gita. In this sense, Dharma is not a universally applicable "law" at all, but highly contextual.

Thiruvalluvar's ideas apply equally to all sections of human society. He teaches that the path of love, grace, knowledge, character, and discipline lead to a life of Aram. Some of his core ideas are described in the following sections.

Equality of Birth

For Valluvar, we are all created in the same way by our mothers. All humans are equal by virtue of birth. Birth into a certain class, caste, tribe, or religion does not grant greatness. "High and low status cannot be accorded at birth," says Valluvar (maxim 972).

We have different vocations. Skills at work and contributions to society differ from person to person, and only some people achieve greatness. Not every politician is a Kamarajar, who was the soul of integrity. He started public schools, employed teachers, built dams, and laid the foundations of a modern Tamil state. Not every medical man is a Dr. Edward Jenner, who invented the first smallpox vaccine. However, even two children from the same mother have different accomplishments and achieve different levels of greatness. Valluvar states that professional skills could be one determinant of greatness (Desigar 1983). For example, not every doctor is as great as Jonas Salk, who developed the polio vaccine. Valluvar's poem says:

பிறப்பொக்கும் எல்லா வுயிர்க்கும் சிறப்பொவ்வா
செய்தொழில் வேற்றுமை யான் (972)

Birth is common to all – vocational
skills make us different.

Manu's Dharmasastra has diametrically opposite views:

- ❖ "But for the sake of the prosperity of the worlds he caused the Brahmana, the Kshatriya, the Vaisya, and the Sudra to proceed from his mouth, his arms, his thighs, and his feet" (1.31).

- ❖ "A Brahmana, coming into existence, is born as the highest on earth, the lord of all created beings, for the protection of the treasury of the law" (1.99)

- ❖ "Whatever is contained in this world is all the property of the Brahmana; the Brahmana verily deserves all by virtue of his superiority and noble birth," claims Manu (1.100).

- ❖ Manu also says, "If a once-born person (Sudra) insults a twice-born one with gross abuse, he should suffer the cutting off of his tongue as he is of low origin" (8.270)

Manu's Dharmasastra also specifies that the names given to children at birth should be based on caste. "The name of the Brahmana should be auspicious, that of the Kshatriya connected with power, that of the Vaishya associated with wealth; while that of the Sudra should be contemptible (2.31)."

Education Uplifts

Valluvar wrote that even if he is born into a higher caste or belongs to a higher stratum of society, a person without learning, an ignorant person, shall not be considered great. An ignorant person, though born into a high caste, is not equal in dignity to a learned person, though the latter may have been born into a low caste. (409):

> மேற்பிறந்தார் ஆயினும் கல்லாதார் கீழ்ப்பிறந்தும்,
> கற்றார் அனைத்திலர் பாடு (குறள் - 409)

> Social origin is irrelevant – the wise gain fame
> while the uneducated stagnate at any stratum.

Thirukkural values education and is critical of illiteracy. Additionally, Valluvar says that a beautiful person without learning and knowledge is like a well-made, attractive, eye-catching toy. Such a person's wealth can be harmful because though he may be pleasing in appearance, he has not been purged of undesirable animal qualities.

Manu, however, says, "A Brahmin, whether learned or ignorant, is a powerful divinity" (9.317).

Manu's Dharmasastra may be studied with care and duly taught to pupils by the learned Brahmana—but not by anyone else (1.103). Education, or learning about the laws, was not accessible to Sudras.

Sharing Wealth

Selfishness is denounced by Valluvar. His Aram considers eating alone without feeding the needy more undesirable than begging.

இரத்தலின் இன்னாதது மன்ற நிரப்பிய
தாமே தமியர் உணல்   (229)

More bitter than begging – filling up coffers
and eating alone.

Manu's Dharmasastra insists on not feeding a Sudra even leftovers (4.80). "A Brahmana shall not offer advice to a Sudra, nor the leavings, nor what has been prepared as an offering to the Gods. He shall not expound the law to him; nor shall he indicate to him any penance" (4.80).

Regard for Farming

Agriculture, though onerous, is the best form of labor; for people, though they go in search of several types of employment, must finally take up farming. Kural says,

உழுதுண்டு வாழ்வாரே வாழ்வார்மற் றெல்லாம்
தொழுதுண்டு பின்செல் பவர் (1033)

They live well who live by farming – the rest follow and honor them for food.

Manu says, "People think agriculture to be good; but that occupation is despised by the righteous; the iron-tipped wood injures the earth and the earthly creatures" (10.84).

'Even if some Brahmins and Kshatriyas practiced trade for livelihood, farming as a profession would need bodily effort and the help of others; so, it shall not be pursued,' says Manu. There is a stone inscription in Achalpuram (in Thanjavur district of Tamil Nadu) that was written during the fourteenth year of Rajaraja II's rule. It deals with the village council's decision forbidding a Brahmin to plough the field using a bull. The effect of this decree persisted up to the 20th century; even in 1921, two Brahmins who pursued agriculture were expelled from their caste. These farmers went to see the Kumbakonam Shankaracharya to make a voluntary offering, after which they were ostracized (Maharasan 2021).

Speaking the Truth

"Not uttering lies is the highest virtue; one may not always have to follow other virtuous paths. Not telling lies yields highest benefit," says Valluvar in maxim 297.

பொய்யாமை பொய்யாமை ஆற்றின் அறம்பிற
செய்யாமை செய்யாமை நன்று   (297)

I Iold firmly against falsehood – no
other virtue surpasses this.

Vasistha Dharmasutra allows lying in special cases if
needed (chapter 16.35):

Men may speak an untruth at the time of marriage, during a
dalliance, when their lives are in danger, when the loss of
their whole property is imminent, and for the sake of a
Brahmana; they declare that an untruth spoken in these five
cases would not make (the speaker) an outcast.

Killing of Animals

Valluvar considers that abstaining from killing animals and
eating their flesh is better than performing a thousand
oblations in the sacrificial fire:

அவிசொரிந்து ஆயிரம் வேட்டலின் ஒன்றன்

உயிர்செகுத்து உண்ணாமை நன்று (குறள் 259)

Not taking and eating a single life – better than
a thousand offerings through fire.

"The eater incurs no sin by eating, even daily, such animals
as are eatable: since the eater as well as the eaten animals
have been created by the creator himself" (Manu 5.30).

Path to Wisdom

Valluvar believed that the path to righteousness, Aram, is
about gaining knowledge and becoming wise. Toward this
end, a person need not blindly accept anybody's views or
words. Regardless of the subject matter and the source of
information, he encourages us to seek the truth. The author
encourages us to ask questions. Similarly, Lord Buddha
wrote, "Do not believe in anything simply because you have
heard it. Do not believe in anything simply because it is
spoken and rumored by many. Do not believe in anything
simply because it is found written in your religious books.

Do not believe in anything merely on the authority of your teachers and elders. Do not believe in traditions because they have been handed down for many generations. But after observation and analysis, when you find that anything agrees with reason and is conducive to the good and benefit of one and all, then accept it and live up to it."

எப்பொருள் யார்யார்வாய்க் கேட்பினும்

அப்பொருள்
மெய்ப்பொருள் காண்ப தறிவு (423)

To discern the real truth from whatever source it emanates is the true quality of wisdom.

Dharmasastra and related texts were beyond criticism, and anybody refusing to accept the Vedas and Smritis were termed Nastika (Shrimad Bhagavatam Canto 4.2.30). Chaitanya Mahaprabhu went on to term Buddhists as Nastika. He says, 'In order to establish his doctrine of nonviolence, Lord Buddha flatly refused to believe in the

Vedas, and thus later on, Shankaracharya stopped this system of religion and forced it to go outside India."

Aram conveys the opposite: question, examine the veracity of what is said, and gain wisdom.

Justice without Bias

Without taking sides, after conducting a thorough, neutral investigation of the fault or crime to find the culprit, the king delivers justice based only on the crime (541)

ஓர்ந்து கண்ணோடாது இறைபுரிந்து யார்மாட்டும்
தேர்ந்து செய்வதே முறை   (541)

Test and evaluate impartially
Consult and implement the laws justly.

If a low-born person intentionally harasses a Brahmana, the King shall strike him with various fearsome forms of corporal punishment (9.248). Manu seeks exemption for Brahmanas even if they are found guilty of murder:

"There is no greater crime on earth than the slaying of a Brahmana; the king shall, therefore, not even think of his death in his mind" (8.381).

Righteousness at Any Cost

A person might be pushed into poverty and therefore unable to fulfill the basic needs of an aging mother. For a grown-up son or daughter, seeing his or her mother hungry would be difficult to bear. Thirukkural (656) conveys that even in such a situation, one must not stray from the path of righteousness set by wise men. We are tacitly asked to keep away from lying, stealing, accepting bribes, and cheating to feed the mother. It is a noble ideal and duty to not let our own near and dear go without food, but it is nobler not to indulge in any activity that will violate the "code of righteousness."

ஈன்றாள் பசிகாண்பான் ஆயினுஞ் செய்யற்க

சான்றோர் பழிக்கும் வினை   (656)

Though you may have to watch your mother
starve

Do nothing that the noble condemn.

The above ideas of Aram are different from the "all is fair in love and war" dictum that we see in the Ramayana and Mahabharata that is hedged in by many explanations, justifications, contradictions, and sermons. Sanatana Dharma as expounded by the Sastras had a goal, and its ethical model of Dharma is based on a hierarchical society divided by caste. Valluvar uses a different model of society that bases ethics on the equality of all humans. We will see more of this divergence as we read the book further.

Chapter 3

Rain: Worship, Charity, and Penance

After opening the book by praising the divine, Valluvar glorifies rain. He declares that rain is an elixir. The world survives and thrives on rain. Water is an essential food and serves as an input for all life on Earth. Not even a blade of grass can survive without rain. If rains fail, farmers cannot grow and cultivate crops. We will all starve. Virtue, wealth, and pleasure will cease to exist on this planet.

For Valluvar, "those who lead a righteous life in this world will be ranked among the saints (*theyvams*) in the heavenly skies" (50). It is love, compassion, and purity of heart that make human beings great, that is, worthy of being honored with divinity in the heavens.

Many of our ancients celebrated and remembered their exemplary ancestors. They believed that our ancestors gained admittance to heaven (வானோர்) based on their virtuous deeds. If the clouds run dry (வறக்கு), the rains are bound to fail. Valluvar notes that when the rains fail, even festivities, worship, and celebrations centering around remembering our ancestors cannot take place (18).

Festivities, remembrances, and celebrations were centered on the prosperity associated with cultivation and yield. If the rains fail, what will we have to offer in festivities and celebrations? We celebrate prosperity. We offer our gratitude as prayers accompanied by charity.

சிறப்பொடு பூசனை செல்லாது வானம்

வறக்குமேல் வானோர்க்கும் ஈண்டு (18)

Festive prayers for celestials do not happen
when the skies fail and the earth lies
barren.

Even today we observe these festivities as a mark of gratitude to our ancestors. Special worship (சிறப்பொடு பூசனை) is associated with celebrations. In our celebrations, we offer fine produce from our fields. When clouds run dry and the rains fail, the harvest will also fail, and the accompanying drought will curb joyful celebrations and festivities. Hence, rain is even tied to our spiritual well-being.

தானம் தவம் இரண்டும் தங்கா

வியன்உலகம்

வானம் வழங்கா தெனின் (19)

Charity and Penance cease – when

the skies do not provide.

Valluvar says that if the rains fail, "Charity and Penance may not be sustained." The spiritual activities of charity and penance have been carried out across cultures in human history. A portion of the wealth obtained by righteous means is donated for good causes such as feeding the poor and devotees in temples. As acts of grace, people help the poor with donations, funding educational institutions, hospitals, and shelters.

People all over the world practice charity and penance. Charity is rendering voluntary assistance in the form of money, food, or other physical means, and even by spending time with the needy.

Penance involves fasting, prayers, pilgrimage, wearing simpler clothing, and even denying ourselves material pleasures at times. People may abstain from alcohol, smoking, meat, and in modern times even television screens and other forms of entertainment. The practice of penance may involve mastering ourselves to build our strength in order to prepare ourselves for the trials and tribulations in life. Most commentators consider penance a self-effacing act carried out by laypersons.

Valluvar talks about remembrance of ancestors, prayers, offerings, special celebrations, and penance. In these maxims, he does not identify himself with any specific religion. Penance, prayers, charity, and celebrations take place in all religions and civilizations. Many Orthodox Christians fast during Great Lent. Muslims fast during the month of Ramzan. Pilgrimages to Mecca and holy sites are similar to pilgrimages to Kashi, the Himalayas, and Palani.

In *Thirukural: An Abridgement of Sastras*, the author, Nagaswamy, claims that Valluvar associates penance (Thavam) exclusively with Hindu mendicants who follow the Upanishads. The author uses selective interpretation when he writes: "Thavam is something foreign to Christian concepts. Hindus observe a strict code to achieve something greater, not for expiation; but as a pathway to redemption (moksha)."

To someone who is captivated by fantastic mythology, Thavam may generate images that show the practitioner sleeping alone in a forest, unmindful of the rain, snow, and heat of the sun; walking on water; and performing rituals and exercises to obtain boons from the divine. The person practicing Thavam may live alone on a mountain, sleep in a solitary cave, and magically develop the ability to bestow boons with blessings or inflict suffering with curses (Desigar 1983).

Now, Valluvar does not give ascetics or people of a certain faith exclusive proprietary rights to Thavam (penance). Valluvar defines and describes penance in many places.

Thiruvalluvar's treatment of penance is innovative and simple. Penance comes naturally to those who conduct themselves with love and practice charity. Patiently tolerating one's own suffering and not harming others is the essence of penance (261):

உற்ற நோய் நோன்றல் உயிர்க்குறுகண்
செய்யாமை

அற்றே தவத்திற்கு உரு (261)

Enduring pain, like fasting, and abjuring
injury

To other lives are facets of penance.

The life of a householder is held in exceedingly high esteem in Thirukkural. Valluvar does not limit the attainment of sainthood (நோன்மை) to people who leave their homes to be ascetics. A domestic householder who does not swerve from righteousness and guides his family, kith, and kin along the virtuous path is held in high regard as well; his life can be saintlier than that of a saint. In maxim 48, the poet says:

ஆற்றின் ஒழுக்கி அறனிழுக்கா

இல்வாழ்க்கை

நோற்பாரின் நோன்மை உடைத்து (48)

Domestic life that guides people along the righteous path,

is saintlier than the life of a saint.

A householder not only sustains ascetics, the elderly, his parents, and family members; he is also duty bound to raise his children well and educate them so that they can hold their own in a gathering of the learned (67). Valluvar also talks about the help a child can render a parent in return:

மகன் தந்தைக்கு ஆற்றும் உதவி

இவன்தந்தை

என்னோற்றான் கொல்எனும் சொல் (70)

The help a child can render a parent is to
gain recognition,

so that people wonder, "What penance did
the parent do to bear him?"

He refers to penance again in maxim 70. The world may
wonder about the perseverance and determination of the
parent in raising a child who conducts herself well and gains
honor. A child brought up well by her parents will become
a noble citizen. He will help his hometown and the world
with his virtue, intelligence, and talent. He will be praised
by people as a person of good standing.

If a father wants his son to become a good, successful
citizen, he will nurture him with determination, inspiring
him to strive hard to become an achiever. Only then will
that son advance to great heights. Valluvar also refers to this

process by which a parent raises an exemplary child as a facet of penance.

In conclusion, Valluvar says that the skies gift rain to enable life to flourish amid an abundance of food and prosperity on Earth. The well-being enabled by rain is also necessary to sustain offerings, charity, and penance. Penance practiced by the virtuous involves the ability to tolerate suffering and refraining from harming any living being. Many facets of penance are described by Valluvar without limiting the idea to any particular scriptural, religious, or parochial practice.

Chapter 4

Learning, Education, and Knowledge

To analyze Valluvar's contribution to the ideals of learning, knowledge, and wisdom, we need to first describe the background of the education system of his time. The main school system that existed in the Indian subcontinent was called *gurukul*. The gurukul was actually the home of the teacher or *acharya* and was the center of learning. Pupils resided in the gurukul until their education was complete. The student had to offer a *gurudakshina*, which was a token of respect paid to the teacher. It was mainly in the form of money or a special task that the student had to perform for the teacher.

However, the gurukul system was parochial in its admission process. Brahmin, Kshatriya, and Vaishya students were admitted to the gurukul at the ages of six, eight, and eleven, respectively. It was called Yajnopavita/Upanayana (or Upavita then), and sacrificial rituals were performed before the students were admitted.

Sudras and women were not admitted to gurukuls. It should be clearly understood that ancient education operated under these severe limitations.

Valluvar places his ideas on learning and education on a timeless plane. Unlike the message of the Sastras, his message has a modern flavor and is valid even today. Any form of discrimination is anathema to him. He does not place any limitations on learning and the learner. He declares emphatically that letters and numbers are the two eyes of all humans (392). Valluvar's call for learning numbers and letters as a vision for all human beings is echoed even now. Dr. Kofi Anan, former Secretary-General of the United Nations, said, "Education is a human right with immense power to transform. On its foundation rest the cornerstones of freedom, democracy, and sustainable human development." The period when Valluvar wrote about the importance of numbers was technologically naive. Traders and craftsmen of his days would have used basic arithmetic. Most of the advances in the sciences occurred after the development of calculus and advanced math in the 17th century. In today's advanced world, testing in math and language skills is used to assess students.

One can get protection from enemies by calling in the police, by using one's own physical strength, by tapping into one's network of connections, and even by using the law. Valluvar viewed knowledge as a shield against both one's faltering will and enemies. Knowledge is a tool that builds inner confidence and motivation, keeping us aware of our surroundings. Enemies can easily destroy a fort built of stones, rock, mortar, and metal, but they cannot easily destroy the fort of knowledge:

அறிவு அற்றம் காக்கும் கருவி செறுவார்க்கும்

உள்ளழிகல் ஆகா அரண் (421)

Knowledge, the tool that guards against ruin;

the fortress that falls to no enemy.

He stresses the importance of questioning to find the truth and gives primacy to reason (423). Valluvar's learner is unfazed by any statement made by anyone. He is willing to question the validity of any assertion by checking its veracity and validity. In a sense, Valluvar encourages the reader to question even his own verses. Like a scientist who develops hypotheses and discovers the truth using experiments, Valluvar insists on self-inquiry:

எண்ணென்ப ஏனை எழுத்தென்ப இவ்விரண்டும்

கண்ணென்ப வாழும் உயிர்க்கு　(392)

The two – numbers and letters – are the eyes

of living beings.

எப்பொருள் யார்யார்வாய்க் கேட்பினும்

அப்பொருள்

மெய்ப்பொருள் காண்ப தறிவு (423)

Whatever anyone may say, discerning

its truth is knowledge.

Learning is a lifelong process. Our knowledge grows in proportion to our learning. Valluvar conveys this beautifully in maxim 396. Water will flow from a well in proportion to the depth to which it is dug; likewise, our knowledge will grow in proportion to our learning. Here, he uses the metaphor "dig deep" to convey the idea of augmenting one's learning. The poet tacitly underscores the role of hard work in seeking knowledge, which accumulates when one learns more and more. This maxim is very poetic and rich in metaphors. As we immerse ourselves in the act of learning, knowledge oozes out. Water oozes into the well; we can draw or tap into it, and the source replenishes itself. Education and learning are activities that we can immerse ourselves in, and knowledge oozes out similar to how water can be tapped in the well.

The poet also wonders why people are not pursuing education when a learned person can go to any country and live in any town (397). He talks about lifelong learning, learning until the end of life. Learning, even in today's context, is not just about earning degrees; it is about keeping up with changes and newer trends, growing and updating our knowledge so that we do not find even a change of terrain or nation unsettling. Age need not end our learning; it does not limit our need to update our knowledge. We may have to learn a new language and new laws. We may have to update our licenses. As the poet conveys not just a change in town but also a country, he sees education (learning) as a tool to bridge even cultural gaps. Today, learning confers mobility, and people with education and learning who are displaced due to economic hardships or war find it easier to settle down in their new environs.

தொட்டனைத் தூறும் மணற்கேணி மாந்தர்க்கு

கற்றனைத் தூறும் அறிவு (396)

To the depth a person digs, a well fill – to the depth a person learns, a mind deepens.

யாதானும் நாடாமால் ஊராமால் என்னொருவன்

சாந்துணையுங் கல்லாத வாறு (397)

It makes all places one's home and country – why wouldn't a man learn until he dies.

Nagaswamy, in his book *Thirukural: An Abridgement of Sastras*, without even touching on any of these maxims, provides an "equivalent" Sastra from Kautilya. He quotes only one maxim (391) from the chapter on learning. In the following maxim, Valluvar talks about abiding by and practicing flawlessly what is learned:

கற்க கசடறக் கற்பவை கற்றபின்

நிற்க அதற்குத் தக (391)

Faultlessly learn what is to be learned – then let your conduct flow from your learning.

Nagaswamy touches on this very first maxim on learning (on page 138 of his book) but fails to cite any match from the Sastras for the rest of the chapter. He refers to Arthasastra and writes, "Sciences should be studied under qualified teachers and the precepts duly followed. Discipline is the fruit of learning." Maxim 391 of Valluvar does not specify science or any particular subject. Further, our poet does not talk about discipline. Valluvar emphasizes flawless learning and the ability to put learning into practice in real life.

In summary, the chapter on learning written by Valluvar has ten couplets that are studded with some gems, which we have discussed. The poet encourages questioning to seek the truth, acquire knowledge, and put learning into practice. Knowledge is exalted as a shield against ruin. He conveys the lessons that learning helps us bridge cultural gaps and that knowledge grows with learning. Nagaswamy cites only one Sastra to support his abridgment thesis, which does not pass muster on even the topic of education and learning. He needs to find more than one maxim and much more material from the Sastras to establish his "abridgment" thesis.

Chapter 5

Hospitality: The Householder's Lofty Virtue

Valluvar describes the responsibilities of the householder, according high respect to people leading a family life. He asserts that a married family person serves as a support to his immediate circle of friends and family. Hospitality is one of the traits he idealizes in the householder. Hospitality characterizes the ideal relationship between a guest and a householder, who is expected to receive and entertain the guest—whether a known person or a stranger—with goodwill. Chevalier Louis de Jaucourt describes hospitality in the Encyclopédie (a general encyclopedia published in France between 1751 and 1772) as the virtue of a great soul whose ties of humanity move him to care for the whole universe.

Thiruvalluvar begins his chapter on hospitality by describing the objective of earning wealth and maintaining a home. Most would say that this purpose is to provide food and shelter for the family. However, Thiruvalluvar's counterintuitive formulation of this purpose is lofty: he stresses that the purpose of earning wealth and maintaining a home is to provide hospitality to guests. One may wonder if this would not dissipate the wealth of the householder. Valluvar, however, is persuasive: he reassures the householder that he will attain bliss and that his benevolence will put him beyond the reach of poverty or pain. The householder may have a guest waiting at his doorstep. He may possess the food of celestials (ambrosia) that will give his family immortality. Even then, Valluvar would like the host to share the ambrosia with the guest. Maxim 82 advocates the sharing of even ambrosia with guests.

A similar sentiment about sharing ambrosia, the divine nectar, was also expressed in Tamil before Thiruvalluvar. "People with character, even when they get the food of celestials, will not eat alone without sharing it," wrote the Pandya King Ilamvaluthi in Purananuru (182).

விருந்து புறத்ததாத் தானுண்டல் சாவா
மருந்தெனினும் வேண்டற்பாற் றன்று (82)

With a guest at the door: even it be the nectar of
the gods, eating alone is reprehensible.

அமிழ்தம் இயைவ தாயினும் இனிதெனத்
தமியர் உண்டலும் இலரே (புறநா 182.2-3)

Exemplary men may even get Ambrosia,

but do not claim it for themselves.

(Puram, 182, lines 2-3)

The message conveyed by Valluvar is that the guest
deserves to be served the best that the host possesses.
Moreover, the guest should be served first. In his book
Thirukural: An Abridgement of Sastras, the author,
Nagaswamy, quotes a Sastra from Manusmriti that he feels
was the source of Valluvar's idea. Let us see what Manu
says.

On page 129 of his book, Nagaswamy says, "Similar ideas
are found in the Dharmasastra (3.117-118): A householder is

to partake of the food remaining after he has fed the gods, sages, guests, manes, and household deities. He who prepares food for the sake of self simply eats the sin."

In maxim 82, Valluvar does not talk about gods, sages, and deities. He does not invoke any sin. He simply says that even if the householder possesses ambrosia that will give him immortality, it must be served to the guest. This is a positive, secular message uncolored by fear or religious sentiment. Further, if Valluvar's work is an abridgment of the Sastras, the ideas would need to be identical. Valluvar's chapter on hospitality has maxims other than the one cited by Nagaswamy that do not have equivalent sentiments in the Sastras.

Valluvar captivates the reader with the vividness of his imagery in some of his couplets. He also shows a deep understanding of human psychology. He probably had experienced inhospitality as a guest and registered it as an unpleasant memory. He captures the feelings of a rebuffed guest with a memorable metaphor. Anichcham (*Anagallis arvensis*) is a flower that has very soft petals. Just smelling the flower is enough to cause its delicate petals to wilt. The poet uses this wilting of the petals in analogy with the feelings of a guest confronting a cold host. Just as the Anichcham flower wilts when we try to enjoy its fragrance by smelling it, the unwelcoming face of the host will wither away the joy of the guest (90).

மோப்பக் குழையும் அனிச்சம் முகந்திரிந்து
நோக்கக் குழையும் விருந்து (90)

Anichcham flowers wilt when smelt – a guest

wilts when the face of the host turns sour.

Maxim 90, for example, does not have any equivalent in the Sastras. On the strength of one maxim (maxim 82) and a quote from the Dharmasastra that—despite a fake similarity—actually differs from the sentiment expressed by Valluvar in that maxim, Nagaswamy claims that

Thirukkural is an abridgment of Sastras. This is devoid of elementary logic, leave alone scholarly integrity.

Chapter 6

The Exemplar: Valluvar's Model Citizen

The greatest and most intense theme of Valluvar's work is focused on what he calls Aram: a path through life that when followed and a set of virtues that when practiced by a family man will make his life on Earth noble enough for him to take his place alongside heavenly dwellers. Valluvar deals with the set of qualities and characteristics that a person should possess to be considered a Sanron.

English does not have a word that is the exact equivalent of Sanron. Translators have used a range of words to describe a Sanron. I find *exemplar* to be the most suitable equivalent. Let us call Valluvar's exemplar a Sanron. The English word *exemplar* has French and Latin roots denoting a model of virtue.

Before we build up the character model that eventually manifests itself as a Sanron, we can ponder a maxim where Valluvar expresses the intense joy of a mother when she hears her child being hailed as a Sanron. This maxim is often quoted in schools to motivate children to live up to ideals:

ஈன்ற பொழுதின் பெரிதுவக்கும் தன்மகனைச்

சான்றோன் எனக்கேட்ட தாய்   (69)

A mother rejoices even more than at his birth,

upon hearing that her son is considered a Sanron.

The mother who hears her son called a Sanron will rejoice more than she did at his birth.

I sought out echoes from both modern science and mothers. The intensity of the joy that a woman experiences when she first becomes a mother is indescribable. Modern neuroscience has discovered the activity of the brain that brings joy to the mother.

This Kural is a masterpiece. We know that Valluvar is unambiguous about equality of birth (972). He does not accord a higher status to a child on account of superior family standing or wealth. Character development occurs only as the child grows. The poet's exemplar possesses five qualities: affection, fear (of sin), dutiful benevolence, charity, and truthfulness (Kural 983). Interestingly, the person's economic or social status does not come into play; even formal education or positions held are irrelevant:

அன்புநாண் ஒப்புரவு கண்ணோட்டம்
வாய்மையொடு
ஐந்துசால் ஊன்றிய தூண்   (983)

Love, truth, regard, modesty, and grace

are the five pillars that uphold exemplary

character.

Now let us see how the author of *Thirukural: An Abridgement of Sastras* treats Kural 69. After quoting couplet 69 on page 188 of his book, the author says:

"This too finds an echo in the Sastras: it states that the son who upholds by his intellect, virtues, strength, wealth, and the name of the family, only by him do the mother truly attain motherhood."

An echo is a true reflection. The word *Sanron* is unique in representing five qualities, none of which have anything to do with wealth, family, or even intellect. Valluvar describes the unique joy a mother feels on hearing her child called Sanron, a joyous moment that is not mentioned in the Sastras. Her child's family name, wealth, and strength do not make Valluvar's mother rejoice; the model child is a Sanron who possesses affection, the grace of charity, the fear of sin, dutiful benevolence, and truthfulness. We can conclude that the echo of the Sastras detected by Nagaswamy in Kural 69 is a figment of his imagination.

Chapter 7

Anthanars and Brahmins: Are they Different?

Most Sanskritologists deny that from Sangam times Tamils had developed their own culture and language independently of major Vedic influences. They do not want to delve into the Tamil tradition; instead, they jump into Kural and start cherry-picking verses to fit their ideological worldview.

One such example is the concept of Anthanar in Tamil. Sanskritologists immediately conclude that Anthanars are synonymous with Brahmins. In fact, Tamil Anthanars could belong to any caste. They were wise men who often left their families to serve the common folk. They carried old texts and books to study, an umbrella to protect them from the hot sun, a walking stick if they were old, and a mat to sleep on when they traveled the country, eating whatever food was served by the people. Tolkaappiyar, the ancient grammarian of Tamil, clearly defines an Anthanar as follows:

நூலே கரகம் முக்கோல் மணையே

ஆயும் காலை அந்தணர்க் குரிய

Texts on ethics, a pot, a three-section staff, and a matted seat
when we analyze, belong to Anthanar (virtuous).

Some Sanskrit revisionists get excited on seeing the word *nool* (i.e., thread) and immediately define the word *Anthanar* as a holy-thread-wearing Brahmin. There are many references to Tamil sages carrying small pots (*karakam* or *karaNdai*) tied to ropes in *Manimekalai* and *Kaliththokai.*

In the chapter of Thirukkural, "The Greatness of Ascetics," he describes Anthanar as truly virtuous, because in their conduct toward all creatures, they are the embodiment of kindness.

அந்தணர் என்போர் அறவோர்மற் றெவ்வுயிர்க்கும்

செந்தண்மை பூண்டொழுக லான் (30)

Toward all that breathe, with seemly graciousness they behave;

and thus, to the virtuous, the name of "Anthanar" we give.

We cannot limit people who are blessed with a fine sense of righteousness and grace to categories such as clan, caste, country of origin, and linguistic background. Kind-hearted people who practice virtue hail from all walks of life. They could be men or women, saints, or householders. These people, men or women, of any caste, creed, and nationality, practice kindness and behave graciously with all living beings. People who cannot practice virtue, kindness, and grace cannot be Anthanars.

Right in the preface, Nagaswamy, the author of *Thirukural: An Abridgement of Sastras*, claims that Valluvar's Kural is based on the concept of the Vedas and the Sastras. He takes Kural 8: "Great one, ocean of virtue and compassion, join his feet to swim the sea of vice" and concludes that unless one takes refuge at the feet of the Brahmana men who hold

the chakra of Dharma, it is difficult to "cross the world.
" The word Anthanar is thus hijacked to refer to a Vedic Brahmin.

Any student of Tamil would know that Valluvar did not assign castes based on birth. His Kural 972 asserts the equality of human birth; differences in greatness are achieved only by acquired skills and character.

> பிறப்பொக்கும் எல்லா உயிர்க்கும் சிறப்பொவ்வா
> செய்தொழில் வேற்றுமை யான் (972)

> Birth is common to all – Greatness
> achieved by vocational skills is not.

After erroneously deducing that Anthanars refer to Brahmin men, Nagaswamy proceeds to assume that everything in Thirukkural is derived from the Vedas and the caste system. For an example of this, consider the following kural:

> அந்தணர் நூற்கும் அறத்திற்கும் ஆதியாய்
> நின்றது மன்னவன் கோல் (543)

> The sage's scripture and virtue spring
> from the scepter of a stately king.

Valluvar stresses that a ruler who is just and fair is also the basis for the learning and virtue of an Anthanar. The poet is of the view that fair governance is needed for the kind-hearted and virtuous to thrive. Under a despot or dictator, even the virtuous are not protected. They cannot go about freely writing about, and educating people about, good values. Their teachings and works may be banned. An able ruler will not be afraid to let Anthanars do their work even though he may not agree with their teachings. A just ruler will thus enable Anthanars to carry out their work freely.

Nagaswamy's interpretation of this Kural, which he presents on page 148 of his book, is a complete fallacy. He sees a parallel between the above couplet and Arthasastra 1.3, which he interprets as follows: "The state is disciplined by the established laws of the Aryans, which is rooted in the organization of castes and orders, and protected by three Vedas, progresses and never deteriorates."

Valluvar's Kural (543) has nothing to do with castes and the social order (castes). To see a parallel between this Kural and Arthasastra is akin to squaring the circle. In short, Valluvar's Anthanar is a learned person who is compassionate and kind to all living beings. No specific caste is assigned to such a person. Valluvar stresses the importance of the ruler's scepter as the basis of the learning and virtue of an Anthanar. This has no parallel in the Sastras, which held rigid views about the caste hierarchy. Manusmriti always placed the Brahmin above the king — especially a Sudra king. Chhatrapati Shahu Maharaj has left evidence of the Brahmin's grip on the state (Ilaiah 2021). It is well known that he was a Sudra king who was committed to the development of all citizens.

We have seen how the word *Anthanar* has been used historically to refer to ascetics and not to any particular caste. Nagaswamy examines a few commentaries and translators of Kural such as Pope, Lazarus, V. Ramachandra Dikshitar, K. Bala, and Vanmika to find a suitable narrative. He summarizes his findings on pages 78–79 of his book. Only one author, Dikshitar, refers to the Anthanar as a

Brahmin. Nagaswamy holds on to that, saying "avoiding the word *Brahmin* for Anthanar is unwarranted."

He states that "Valluvar held Brahmins with the highest respect; his esteem for Brahmanas was severely attacked by Christian missionaries, who wanted to wean away from the population for their sectarian religious conversion in the last 300 years." To strengthen his narrative, he enlists the support of Manu (which is hardly a surprise!). He claims that all Dharmas were entrusted with Brahmana as he was created first, and his duty is to protect all people who follow Dharma.

In Manu's Manav Dharmasastra, we find the following:

- ❖ **1.31.** But for the sake of the prosperity of the worlds, he caused the Brahmana, the Kshatriya, the Vaisya, and the Sudra to proceed from his mouth, his arms, his thighs, and his feet.
- ❖ **1.88.** To Brahmanas he assigned teaching and studying, sacrificing for their own benefit and for others, giving and accepting (of alms).

- ❖ **1.89.** The Kshatriya he commanded to protect the people, to bestow gifts, to offer sacrifices, to study, and to abstain from attaching himself to sensual pleasures.

- ❖ **1.90.** The Vaisya tend cattle, bestow gifts, offer sacrifices, study, trade, lend money, and cultivate the land.

- ❖ **1.91.** One occupation only the lord prescribed to the Sudra, to serve meekly even these (other) three castes.

Nagaswamy is neither the first scholar nor the last one who has found himself on a slippery slope when addressing Thirukkural. To obfuscate the truth, such scholars find a convenient scapegoat in the Dravidian movement, whose agenda is supposedly to revise the commentary on Thirukkural.

Conduct and Brahmanism

Hindu society is hierarchical. Birth into a caste confers social status, which is attributed to its holy texts (Sastras). This status is passed on to children and grandchildren. Because Hindus observe strict caste norms in marriages, a small section of society is exalted and the rest of society is debased – in perpetuity. These texts accord status based on birth. Valluvar emphatically calls for equality of birth (972). Special respect and reverence, according to the poet, are attained by one's deeds. Status is achieved by conduct, excellence in action, and achievements.

பிறப்பொக்கும் எல்லா உயிர்க்கும் சிறப்பொவ்வா
செய்தொழில் வேற்றுமை யான் (972)

Birth is common to all – Greatness
achieved by vocational skills is not.

Valluvar's ideal of society stands out for its clarity. He wrote his verses when the caste system had gained ground in

Tamil lands. Aryan Brahmins, addressed by Tamils as *paarpanar*, had claimed superiority based on birth in their texts. Their claim to this status was based on their purported knowledge of the Vedas. Valluvar underscores the importance of conduct that transcends any recital of scriptures.

In maxim 134, Valluvar says, "A Brahmin (*paarpaan*) can forget his lore; it can be regained. But if his conduct is improper, his exalted state based on birth will be debased."

மறப்பினும் ஒத்துக் கொளலாகும் பார்ப்பான்
பிறப்பொழுக்கங் குன்றக் கெடும் (134)

A Brahmin can recall forgotten lore,
But conduct lost returns no more.

The exalted status accorded to a Brahmin is based on Hindu texts and grounded in claims of birth. Because society was endogamous for thousands of years, the social status of people depended on their birth. Valluvar values status earned by good conduct higher than birth-based status. Now, let us see what Sastras Nagaswamy cites to support the ideas of this maxim.

Nagaswamy quotes Manusmriti (1.109): "A Brahmana who departs from the rule of conduct, does not reap the fruit of the Veda, but he who duly follows it, will obtain the full reward" (1.109).

Valluvar's maxim asserts that high or low status is not based on birth and gives the example of a Brahmin who claims high status based on birth. Manu, however, states that a Brahmin whose conduct is poor will not get the benefits of his recitals; however, good behavior will reward him. Manu talks about the benefits accruing to a Brahmin. Valluvar, however, raises conduct over birth by using the Brahmin caste (*paarpaan*) as an example. Manu does not repudiate the Brahmin's claim of superiority; he merely deals with the fruits of Vedic duty.

Chapter 8

The Light of Truth that Guides Exemplars

We have described earlier how the maxims of Valluvar are connected (see the Appendix for a description of how we can get the big picture by complementation and augmentation). Reading and interpreting a maxim in and of itself yields a sublime message. However, the author has also composed supporting maxims that help illuminate the ideas conveyed by a primary maxim. That is, the author tacitly refers to other maxims to give a more complete picture of some maxims. The reader can understand the idea conveyed on a larger canvas by augmentation (see the Appendix). For example, Valluvar invokes an exemplar (Sanron) in many maxims, but an exemplar is defined in chapter 98. The defining characteristic of an exemplar is a life guided by truth. Valluvar defines truth (veracity) in chapter 29.

For Valluvar, speaking the truth is speech that does not harm anyone (291). Let me now narrate an example from my life. I was faced with a tough choice in 2019. Both my parents were in urgent care: my mother (Amma) had a respiratory infection and had heart trouble as well. My father (Appa), who was active despite his age, had fallen ill; he was not able to move and was in intensive care. My brother, sister-in-law, and I would take turns to see both of them. Appa passed away, and my sister-in-law was informed. We were with Amma, who was on a ventilator. We ran into an "ethical" issue, with a doctor saying that we have to inform my mother. He left the task to us. We decided not to tell her that Appa had passed away. We felt she would not be able to handle the news. It was a very difficult call. Valluvar's maxim allowed me to make peace with our lie. Even falsehood has the nature of truth if it confers a benefit and does not cause harm (292). The doctors, who thought my mother was more seriously ill than my father and gave her a very small chance of surviving, were surprised she came off the ventilator in a week; after two more weeks, she came home. We apologized to her and gave her the sad news; she coped with the loss from a position of strength.

வாய்மை எனப்படுவது யாதெனின் யாதொன்றும்

தீமை இலாத சொலல் (291)

What is truthfulness? It is nothing but utterance
that causes no harm.

பொய்மையும் வாய்மை யிடத்த புரைதீர்ந்த

நன்மை பயக்கும் எனின் (292)

Even falsehood has the character of truth,

if it bestows benefit free from harm.

We see with what a pragmatic and humanistic perspective
Valluvar approaches the idea of speaking the truth. We learn
that falsehood is almost equivalent to truth when the intent
is to do good without harming anyone. He elevates the
virtue of thinking and speaking the truth higher than
practicing penance and charity (295):

மனத்தொடு வாய்மை மொழியின் தவத்தொடு
தானஞ்செய் வாரின் தலை   (295)

IIe who speaks the truth with all his heart is superior to

those who give gifts and practice austerities.

We care about how others perceive us when we step outside our house. We bathe and groom ourselves to make us look presentable. Valluvar emphasizes both internal and external purity. IIe opines that speaking the truth keeps one's mind clean and free of faults and sins. In Valluvar's words, truth cleanses our mind just as water cleanses our body (298). IIere, Valluvar does not agree with the IIindu belief that sins are washed away by taking a dip in the holy Ganga. IIe emphasizes that the real bath that washes away sins is speaking the truth:

புறள்தூய்மை நீரான் அமையும் அகந்தூய்மை
வாய்மையால் காணப் படும்   (298)

External body is purified by water

Purity within comes by being true.

The poet builds an ideal exemplar who possesses a set of characteristic qualities. According to Valluvar, this exemplary nature is built on five pillars: affection, fear (of sin), dutiful benevolence, charity, and truthfulness (Kural 983). He regards truthfulness as the foremost quality. This is how Valluvar augments his maxims. Valluvar's exemplar, Sanron, does not have to belong to any specific religion; he only needs to possess the qualities required of an exemplar.

An exemplar has many admirable qualities and navigates life using truthfulness as the guiding light. For the exemplar, Sanron, it is not external sources of light such as the sun, the moon, and lamps that illuminate his path; rather, it is truthfulness that illuminates his path (299). Valluvar's exemplar is guided by an inner light kindled by the virtue of truth, a light that outshines external sources of light such as the sun, the moon, and lamps.

எல்லா விளக்கும் விளக்கல்ல சான்றோர்க்குப்

பொய்யா விளக்கே விளக்கு   (299)

All of nature's lamps do not illuminate – the lamp of truth

gives radiance to the exemplar.

Maxim 299 has to be studied using the technique of complementation. All the maxims in chapter 29 complement maxim 299 to define and place the guiding light of truth in perspective. At the same time, maxim 299 augments Valluvar's ideal exemplar, who is defined in chapter 98.

On page 134 of his widely publicized book, *Thirukural: An Abridgement of Sastras*, Nagaswamy cites a sloka from the Bhagwad Gita to match maxim 299:

BG 6.19: "Just as a lamp in a windless place does not flicker, so the disciplined mind of a yogi remains steady in meditation on the Supreme."

In this sloka, the steady focus of a trained Yogi is likened to a lamp that does not flicker. Valluvar's lamp is the light of truth that guides the mind of a noble exemplar. These two concepts are completely different. The only common word is lamp. The Yogi in meditation and Valluvar's exemplar (Sanron) are two different people. The lamp Valluvar talks about is Poyyaa Vilakku: the lamp of truth, the lamp that extinguishes the darkness in our minds.

Chapter 9

The Ideal Country: Safety, Wealth, the Leader, and the People

Thirukkural embraces universality. Valluvar's maxims are not parochial; they apply to all of humanity. Many great ancient works of literature are studied today, but they may not apply to today's world and times. However, most of Valluvar's maxims are relevant even today. V.C. Kulandaiswamy in his Sahitya-Academy-award-winning book, *Immortal Kural*, highlights the contemporary relevance of Thirukkural.

Valluvar has devoted a chapter to his ideal of a country. He starts the chapter with the following kural:

தள்ளா விளையுளும் தக்காரும் தாழ்விலாச்
செல்வரும் சேர்வது நாடு   (731)

A country consists of people who reap unfailing harvests, who are virtuous, and who live together with merchants who own inexhaustible wealth.

An ideal country is not defined by a territory and land mass alone. Valluvar emphasizes virtuous people and cultivable soil that yields plentiful produce to feed the people. He also mentions the process that makes it possible to supply the produce to citizens. Having emphasized that food and farmers are the necessary prerequisites for a land of happy people, he adds that people who are qualified, skilled, and just are also required. He desires men who make products and distribute them in a fair manner among fellow citizens, sell them to other countries, and create wealth. He qualifies wealthy men in the maxim as those whose wealth does not diminish (*தாழ்விலாச் செல்வர்*) even though they make generous charitable donations.

பெரும்பொருளால் பெட்டக்க தாகி

அருங்கேட்டால்

ஆற்ற விளைவது நாடு   (732)

An ideal country has abundant wealth, is desired by all,

is rarely affected by calamities, and produces great yield.

Even a country that is full of well-fed people, fair-minded people equipped with skills, and people who create and share wealth can be affected by natural catastrophes. This leads the poet to another ideal for a country: he desires that the country be free from calamities (in maxim 732).

Valluvar has thought about the many ways of sustaining a civilization. Even in modern times, we know that many islands and coastal communities are threatened by hurricanes and sea water rise due to global warming. Some countries such as Cuba have realized the folly of destroying coastal wetlands, which serve as barriers that protect the mainland from the fury of hurricanes. Cuba has been working to minimize calamities by restoring its coastal mangroves, which also filter seawater and prevent salinity in coastal areas. Salinity affects the cultivation of food crops. By replanting mangroves, Cuba has made net gains in recent years (Rodriguez 2014).

As we have seen, Nagaswamy, throughout his work, cherry-picks one or two maxims out of some selected chapters, and tries to find a match in the Sastras. In chapter 73, devoted to "country," he tries to find a match for two maxims in the Sastras and implies that Valluvar borrowed his ideas from them. Nagaswamy quotes the following Sastra as the one that influenced maxims 731 and 732:

> **"A righteous man shall seek to dwell in a village where fuel, water, fodder, sacred fuel, water, fodder, kusa grass, and garlands are plentiful, access to which is easy, where many rich people dwell, which abounds in industrious people and where Aryans form the majority, and which is not easily entered by robbers"** – Baudhayana [page 161].

The Sastra talks about desirable land where an Aryan can settle down; where he can get fodder for his cattle, and even a particular type of grass. The land should have an Aryan majority. This Sastra is about the land desired by a particular sect and does not cover the many ideas that Valluvar conveys in his maxims. Valluvar's ideas are about a country and not about a sect. They apply to all people and transcend time. Valluvar's ideas on food crop yield, wealth, and charity, and even the ability to ward off calamities are not covered by this Sastra. How then could Valluvar take these ideas from Baudhayana as Nagaswamy implies in his book? Nagaswamy also does not cover Valluvar's ideas in the chapter on "country." He does not offer any matching Sastra for the following:

உறு பசியும் ஓவாப் பிணியும் செறு பகையும்
சேரா தியல்வது நாடு   (734)

An ideal country is that which is not afflicted by starvation,

deadly epidemics, and destructive foes.

கேடறியாக் கெட்ட   இடத்தும் வளங்குன்றா
நாடென்ப நாட்டின் தலை (736)

The learned say that the best kingdom is that which knows no evil (from its foes),

and, if harmed (at all), suffers no diminution in its wealth.

Maxim 734 talks about what an ideal country should not be afflicted by: starvation, incurable disease, and enemies that wage war. Shortage of food leads to price increases and resulting hardship. Lack of water and proper soil can lead to shortage of food crops. India had faced these shortages after Independence and solved them through the "green" and "white" revolutions. The country successfully implemented ways to increase food crop production and milk yield to solve the problem of hunger.

Many life-threatening diseases occur due to changes in weather such as excessive heat or cold. Environmental degradation, pollution, and food adulteration can also threaten life. Diseases can spread from animals. Countries react by formulating plans to minimize deaths.

A country can also face threats from foes, who may appear when they sense that the government has become weak. An efficient government develops its defensive capabilities by strengthening its forces and forts, and also builds strong relationships with friendly neighbors. A country can lose its wealth with enemies around and within.

An ideal country should produce bountiful harvests, and it should be free of starvation and endemic disease. It should not fall into bad days; even if it does, it should not suffer from a paucity of resources (wealth). Additionally, a country will not face trouble from foes if it develops friendly neighbors, strong armed forces, and forts.

In conclusion, we find that in just four maxims that we selected out of ten, Valluvar has covered more ideas than the quoted Sastra. Even the first two maxims in question had a more relevant idea – that of a prosperous modern country – than the Sastra quoted by Nagaswamy. The entire chapter on "country" is detailed and comprehensive. In addition to cultivation of crops to feed the people, inexhaustible wealth, men of good standing, and the absence of hunger, foes, and calamities, he also covers other ideas such as willing taxpayers that support the government, rich water sources, and forests and mountains that serve as natural defenses. He also points out the need for the ruler to be a person of character and for citizens to reciprocate by showing love and goodwill toward the ruler.

Chapter 10

How Competent People Act

We studied Valluvar's maxims in school to memorize and quote them. Often, the maxims we studied were not arranged in any particular sequence or plan. We studied and remembered a few hundred of them. Our curiosity about Thirukkural grows as we become older. Some of the maxims we memorized become more meaningful after we acquire some experience of life.

In India, I had very few opportunities to stand in front of an audience and speak. When I became a graduate student in the United States, I was asked to present ideas and speak about my work. I had brought my Thirukkural book with me to the United States. Valluvar's aphorisms on handling the stage and speaking made perfect sense. Valluvar became a guide on many aspects of my life.

I found that Thirukkural is also a terrific book for sound advice on project planning and execution. This became apparent when I started working in the industry, and also began reading the insights into the book of great writers such as Kulandaiswamy and Prabhakaran. Valluvar lived during a time when the bullock cart was the main mode of transport, but he had thought through his ideas and conveyed them in ways that are applicable even to our times, when we can send humans to the moon.

India is witnessing a rather disturbing trend: it is claimed that many ancient literary works in the subcontinent were inspired by the religion of the Vedas and Sastras. We were taught that Valluvar wrote for all sects, all races, all religions, and people. A book by a well-known scholar of temple architecture, Nagaswamy, has gained a lot of media attention. I came across many unsubstantiated claims that Valluvar's entire work is an abridgment of the Sanskrit Sastras. This motivated me to re-read Thirukkural.

We may plan meticulously, write proposals, apply for grants, and work according to our plan — and yet we may not get the desired results. This has happened to me, and I felt sad — all the devices that we had fabricated in the lab were dying. The devices were new, exceedingly small, and I was not handling them carefully. Charges from my fingers "shocked" them and broke the junctions. The clock was ticking on my PhD program. I became too involved in the intricacies of planning my next step and was not feeling motivated to act. It was winter and I had to somehow weather my blues.

My thesis supervisor came and talked to me nicely: "You have done very well. You have completed 90% of the work. All you need is to make the measurements and wrap it up. We need to plan, but not just get stuck and be too fearful. I would like you to 'Just do it', as the Nike ad says." I needed to summon up all my determination and willpower to execute my alternative plan. Instead of trying to handle the small devices and assemble them on my own fixture, I got an expert to package the devices and designed a fixture to make accurate measurements. I needed an extra boost of confidence and willpower to execute this plan, which proved successful.

Valluvar calls it "Power in Action" – *vinaiththitpam* (வினைத்திட்பம்). He defines it in his first maxim in the chapter:

வினைத்திட்பம் என்பது ஒருவன் மனத்திட்பம்

மற்றைய எல்லாம் பிற (661)

Strength of action has the power to succeed; in its absence all other strengths falter and fail.

"Power in action" is the willpower to execute a task; it is the prerequisite for accomplishing a task.

Valluvar talks about obstacles and motivates us not to sulk in despair; instead, we need to find out ways to remove the obstacles standing in the way of accomplishing the task. People who have "Power in Action" do not easily give up or lose faith when things are not working in their favor.

Although we can translate *vinaiththitpam* (வினைத்திட்பம்) loosely, it is a challenge to express the concept with a few English words. We act to get something done and complete it. Here, we need the idea of substantial (solid) completion;

thitpam (திட்டம்) is thiNNam (திண்ணம்), which denotes definiteness, firmness, and solidity. Action that ends in solid outcomes would be *vinaiththitpam* (வினைத்திட்பம்).

Often, we find people working on a challenging task. They may give updates to their immediate seniors in the company. However, progress is not revealed to the world until it is done and dusted: that is, until the results are positive and the product becomes available. Giving an update to the world and discussing some of the intermediate results would hamper progress and become a distraction, though it would attract temporary attention. Valluvar wants us to fully and solidly complete any piece of work that we undertake and only then announce the results.

He considers this discipline a characteristic trait of accomplished people.

கடைக்கொட்கச் செய்தக்க தாண்மை
இடைக்கொட்கின்
எற்றா விழுமந் தரும்.   (663)

Mastery reveals what is finished --- revelation
in the middle brings misery.

The chapter has wonderful gems about acting so as to
complete a task successfully. I leave it to the reader to learn
more about the chapter and enjoy it. Valluvar's maxims are
written to a poetic meter, and we can sing them too. We
can also enjoy some analogies and metaphors he
introduces now and then. In the chapter "Power in Action,"
he advises us not to underestimate a person's willpower on
the basis of his appearance. A desirable quality of a
manager, or a person in charge of hiring a person for a task,
is not to underestimate or ridicule a person's ability to
complete a difficult task because, for example, the person
is puny. Valluvar uses the analogy of a big chariot wheel
whose function depends on the small lynchpin:

உருவுகண்டு எள்ளாமை வேண்டும்
உருள்பெருந்தேர்க்கு
அச்சாணி அன்னார் உடைத்து (667)

Scorn none for their size ---- there are some

like a pin in a great cart's wheel.

We have studied the importance of power in acting on a task or project. Valluvar has discussed planning, organization, resources, prioritization, and picking the ideal place and time for execution in earlier chapters. The details of his ideas are so intriguing that they are relevant even for our present times. Now, what are Nagaswamy's findings on the ideas expressed in the Sastras about "Power in Action"?

Nagaswamy, on page 156 of his book, quotes two slokas from the Bhagavad Gita (BG) and finds parallels in the chapter "Power in Action" in Thirukkural. Let us examine these slokas and maxims 669 and 670, the last two from the chapter.

BG: 2-3 O Partha, this unmanliness does not befit you. Give up such petty weakness of heart and arise, O vanquisher of enemies.

BG: 4-20 Such people, having given up attachment to the fruits of their actions, are always satisfied and not dependent on external things. Despite engaging in activities, they do not do anything at all.

துன்பம் உறவரினும் செய்க துணிவாற்றி
இன்பம் பயக்கும் வினை (669)

Even in toil enact boldly all action
that ends in joy.

எனைத்திட்பம் எய்தியக் கண்ணும் வினைத்திட்பம்
வேண்டாரை வேண்டாது உலகு (670)

The world does not care about people who lack
the will power to act
despite possessing other strengths.

In just a half a page, Nagaswamy quotes two slokas and finds two maxims from Valluvar which he claims – without any further explanation – are matching "abridgments," leaving the reader clueless. Having been introduced to the chapter on "action" by Valluvar, we are equipped to read the last two kurals and try to analyze the parallelism, if any.

Maxim 669 talks about work or actions that bring about joy when they are successfully completed. Joy is finally achieved. Here, Valluvar motivates us to persist in the actions that will bring joy at the end. The activity may bring a lot of pain, loss, and distress in the short term. However, Valluvar gives us the strength and hope to persist in the face of adversity; he tells us to summon up our commitment and "just do it." Now, how is this the same as Krishna in the Bhagavad Gita literally goading Arjuna to fight the war? Valluvar's *vinai* is the action in question. It applies to the general world, not just war. It could be a project where hurdles have to be overcome before we see the light at the end of the tunnel.

Maxim 670 is about passion and involvement in action. One may have many skills and tools; however, hesitancy and tentativeness in performing a task will not earn one the respect of men of caliber. Other abilities can attract attention and make one noticed for a while. One may be a great speaker. One may be wealthy, attractive, speak well, have many credentials, have friends who are powerful and even connections in high places; these are all strengths too. Valluvar lumps them all in the "Others (எனைத்திட்பம்)" category of strengths. He stresses that the impetus to act (*vinaith_thitpam*) is most valued by society.

The Bhagavad Gita's sloka 4-20 conveys a vastly different idea. It talks about devotion to God. Actions cannot be classified by external appearances. It is the state of the mind that determines what is inaction and action. The minds of enlightened persons are absorbed in God. Being fully satisfied in devotional union with Him, they look upon God as their only refuge and do not depend on external support. In this state of mind, all their actions are termed as *akarm*, or inactions.

Providing a half-page of quotes from the Bhagavad Gita and assuming parallelism between it and Thirukkural is mere wishful thinking. Valluvar's chapter is dedicated to the secular world and stresses resoluteness in action so that a task can be completed successfully. The poet talks about the importance of firmness and focus for completing a planned task or objective despite encountering disappointments, interruptions, and barriers. He motivates the reader by assuring her that tenaciousness in completing the task will bring her joy at the end; the pain and suffering during the journey will not last long. He is careful in using words. As long as the original goal is to bring joy, he insists that one will prevail against setbacks, which will prove to be temporary. Nagaswamy does not have any parallel from the Sastras for these thoughts and therefore resorts to pseudo-random identification of two slokas, quoting them without explanation. Valluvar's chapter is rich in content; it has no fewer than ten maxims. Where are the matching Sastras for the remaining eight maxims?

Chapter 11

Model Citizen's Duty to Society

Social responsibility is an ethical framework in which an individual is obliged to work and cooperate with other individuals and organizations. This will benefit the community that will inherit the world that the individual will eventually leave behind (Jensen 2006). Valluvar recognized the significance of advancing a society through healthy interactions among its citizens. His model citizen possesses the wisdom to show benevolence (ஒப்புரவு அறிதல்) to members of the larger society. In chapter 22, he talks about citizens' awareness of duty to society. The common good takes priority over self-interest, and duty to the larger society is hailed.

The poet likens wealth in the hands of wise men who possess social responsibility to a community well that gets filled with water. Wise men desire that all living forms should flourish. They care about the welfare of the entire world (உலகவாம்). A community well is likened to the wealth of such wise men.

ஊருணி நீர்நிறைந் தற்றே உலகவாம்
பேரறி வாளன் திரு (215)

The wealth of a person with worldly

wisdom is a life-giving well that sustains

a village community.

Valluvar does not spare people who lack social responsibility. He calls them out in maxim 214.

ஒத்தது அறிவான் உயிர்வாழ்வான் மற்றையான்
செத்தாருள் வைக்கப் படும் (214)

Live a fuller life engaged in compatible social service;

otherwise, you'll be considered a corpse.

A human being is a member of the larger society. The needs of society and the role of an individual in it are discerned by wise people. Such a wise person is compatible with society and is regarded a living community well. Otherwise, Valluvar says the person may be considered dead. The wise, who are not simply obsessed with their own possessions and work, become aware of their surroundings and the needs of the people around them. Such persons, who live in harmony with society, have characteristics that make life bloom on this planet. People who lack this understanding are as good as dead even though they may breathe.

The wise person understands that people need food to satisfy their hunger, education to gain knowledge, a residence to gain shelter, and medicine to treat illness. The wise understand this; they want those around them to live well by possessing what they, the wise, have (ஒத்தது அறிவான்). The wise also identify with those around them by empathizing with their grief and sorrows.

One of my friends mentioned that Krishna in the Bhagavad Gita says, "Do your duty. Expect no rewards (fruits)." His position was that the essence of the following kural is the same as Krishna's call:

கைமாறு வேண்டா கடப்பாடு மாரிமாட்டு
என்ஆற்றுங் கொல்லோ உலகு (211)

The benevolent expect no return for
 their dutiful service.
How can the world ever repay the rain cloud?

This maxim appears in the first chapter (chapter 22) on the awareness of duty to society, that is, ஒப்புரவறிதல். This Tamil word conveys the possession of knowledge that enables persons to fulfill their responsibilities as exemplary citizens. We can see that Valluvar's notions of social responsibility and social awareness are different from Arjuna being asked to kill or fight an unjust war for Krishna without expecting rewards. To underscore my point, I narrated the following parable:

Our friend, Thomas, is on his way to work and sees a child that is lost and crying. He comforts her, takes her to the police, stays with her, and waits until her mother has come to pick her up. Meanwhile, he calls his boss and informs him that he will not be able to make it to work. His actions are driven by an instinct; he is aware of his duty to society (ஒப்புரவு). This not the same as a call for killing: "You have to fight, do your duty, but do not concern yourself with the results."

The idea is subtle, but it not difficult to understand if we understand the meaning of the Tamil word. But to understand that we have to listen to the message in the chapter. A person who thinks that everything arises from their sacred text will be deaf to this message. When we act with knowledge of our duty to society, we do so without any expectation of payment or reward. The message "it is your duty to fight this war on my behalf, without expecting any reward in return" is not the same as the message conveyed by Valluvar: knowledge of one's duty to society is the basis of right action.

We need to pay attention to the words in the above maxim and understand the context of the message in the larger scheme of things. In Tamil, *maari* is rain, as in the rain goddess Mariamman. Any act such as the one described above (Thomas finding a lost child on his way to work, comforting her, and staying with her until her mother is found) falls in this category. Here, Valluvar finds an analogy in rain. Rain pours down on the parched land and helps create life on Earth by providing sustenance to many life-forms. Likewise, an enlightened person (i.e., a Sanron: one who is aware of one's duty to society) will respond to situations without expecting any reward. The message conveyed in seven words does need explanation. Even today, people ask, "What *kaimaRu* (recompense; it is not exactly fruit) can I offer for the timely assistance that I received from you?" The first word in maxim 211, *KaimaaRu*, is reciprocation for help received. The poet says, "*KaimaaRu Vendaa*"; that is, no recompense is needed or expected.

Rain does not expect anything back in return. Similarly, the help one offers should not be transactional, that is, the "you scratch my back, and I'll scratch yours" kind of help. I got a Christmas gift from Thomas, and I feel I should give him a gift in return; this is transactional thinking. Action based on an understanding of one's social duty (*oppuravu;* i.e., ஒப்புரவு) is selfless; it is not transactional in spirit. This is what Valluvar says: "*kaimaaRu veNdaa*"; "*kai*" is "hand," "*maaRu*" is "(ex)change." Thus, "*kaimaaRu*" denotes transactional activity. Rain does not expect anything in return for its generosity from the people working on the land. Likewise, an exemplar (a Sanron) will have a sense of *oppuravu* and act.

In conclusion, one cannot look for a few words in a Sastra and try to relate them to translated phrases of Thirukkural. The overall contextual framework of Thirukkural has to be understood. Valluvar uses this chapter to build up the characteristics of his model citizen (this model citizen is an exemplar called Sanron; we addressed this in chapter 6). Blessed with the wisdom to live harmoniously in society and aware of its needs, the model citizen expects no reward for his benevolence. The wealth in his hands is like the water filling a community well; it serves the entire community. The message of the kural in the context of the chapter on duty to society – behave benevolently without expecting anything in return, like rain – is different from the message in the wartime sermon to Arjuna.

Chapter 12

Ethical Wealth Acquisition

Wealth accumulation refers to the acquisition of money, property, or other assets that increase a person's net worth over time. Individuals can acquire wealth by investing and earning returns through their investments. People invest to secure their future financially.

Valluvar provides philosophical underpinnings to the rationale underlying wealth accumulation and the path to wealth acquisition. In this chapter, he starts with the real-world motivation for an individual or a king to accumulate wealth. He also emphasizes the safety and security aspects of savings.

To begin, in maxim 751, he does not mince words when conveying the value and importance of wealth:

பொருளல் லவரைப் பொருளாகச் செய்யும்
பொருளல்லது இல்லை பொருள் (751)

There is nothing like wealth

To make the worthless worthy.

பொருள் அல்லவரை – people who do not have much

value (substance);

பொருளாகச் செய்யும் – make them worthy

பொருள் அல்லது இல்லை – nothing exists but

பொருள் – wealth

There are people who do not possess knowledge, virtue, and talent in arts or sports, but they are still highly regarded, perhaps on account of their wealth. Wealth attracts respect like a magnet and is valuable in and of itself.

We will see the importance of wealth accumulation as conceptualized by Valluvar. He starts the chapter with maxim 751, which is about the reality that a person who has nothing to offer but wealth is held in high regard.

Nagaswamy, who set out to prove that Thirukkural is an abridgment of Sastras, finds a "match" from Ramayana instead of from the often-used alleged parallel, Arthasastra. He quotes a few verses from the forest canto of Ramayana (p. 162) and writes:

❖ "To a man of wealth, there are friends and relatives. He is the worthy man of the world and becomes a Pandita. He is a man of prowess and wisdom. He is a great man with good qualities."

Do we see any match between what Valluvar talks about and the Ramayana verses? Does Valluvar say that a person with wealth also becomes wise, brave, and has great qualities? Our Padma-Bhushan-awarded author evidently did not understand maxim 751, which stresses the importance of wealth even in the absence of other attributes such as wisdom.

The appearance of shared concerns in the literature of different periods does not necessarily imply that one work was influenced by another. For example, hunger has been a concern of human beings since time immemorial. Different writers have addressed the topic of hunger at different times, and many of them drew from direct experience and observation. It would be a grave error of judgment to infer that one author influenced the other.

One of the leading poets in Tamil, Subramania Bharathi, who lived two thousand years after Thiruvalluvar, declared, "Even if one person is deprived of food, we shall destroy the world." This expression of anger at seeing hunger differs from poet to poet. Valluvar even abhorred the practice of begging for food. "May the Creator Himself loiter and perish by wandering about if he has pre-ordained begging too as a means of existence" (1062).

To infer that Bharathi borrowed his idea from Valluvar would be absurd. To try and show that various ideas in Thirukkural were influenced by the Sastras, Nagaswamy often – rather desperately – quotes at random from the former. Valluvar, however, ordered his ideas chapter-wise and developed a whole from the pieces; a chapter consists of individual ideas that complement each other. Without reading the chapter completely and finding a complete maxim-to-maxim match with the Sastras, his thesis cannot be established. Nagaswamy's work did not have to pass the rigorous scrutiny of an academic committee. It was written to deliver what its audience wants to hear, so it is no surprise that scholarly integrity and rigor are conspicuous only by their absence.

Valluvar's chapters are all imbued with virtue (Aram). The idea of Aram pervades his cantos on Wealth (Artha) and Eros (Kama). We saw earlier how Valluvar stresses the significance of wealth and its accumulation. We also saw how the cited Sanskrit Sastra does not match maxim 751.

Conveniently leapfrogging the rest of the maxims in the chapter (752–759), Nagaswamy pounces on the last maxim (760) in chapter 76. The maxim in Tamil:

ஒண்பொருள் காழ்ப்ப இயற்றியார்க்கு
                              எண்பொருள்
ஏனை இரண்டும் ஒருங்கு (760)

Shining wealth well gathered

Attracts the other two.

What does maxim 760 convey? Imagine that we succeeded in creating income-generating channels so that we are now wealthy. This opens up the door for virtuous deeds; we have many ways to do good deeds and follow the righteous path. It also gives us many ways to enjoy the good things of life.

Valluvar depicts the interplay between the three major parts of his "art of living" – virtue, wealth, and joy – in his last maxim of chapter 76. He lays out the connections and does not try to order the three elements – virtue, wealth, and joy – in any specific way. When wealth is obtained, the other two – virtue and joy – are easily realizable. Now, let us look at Nagaswamy's matching Sastra. His choice surprises the serious reader. One would think he would select a match from Kautilya's Arthasastra on wealth acquisition. Interestingly, he resorts to Kamasutra, the adult manual. In chapter 2, verse 18, the author of Kamasutra talks about Virtue, Wealth, and Pleasure, describing the relative importance of these three:

❖ "When all the three, viz, Dharma, Artha, and Kama, come together, the former is better than the one which follows it, i.e., Dharma is better than Artha, and Artha is better than Kama. But Artha is the first that should be practiced by the king, for livelihood of men is to be obtained from that only. Again, Kama being the occupation of public women, they should prefer it to the other two, and these are exceptions to the general rule" – chapter 2-18.

Kamasutra describes a simple hierarchy: Virtue is greater than wealth, which in turn is greater than sex. What does

Valluvar say? If we can earn wealth, the other two – virtue and pleasure – will follow without much trouble. Valluvar does not set up a hierarchy of preference among wealth, virtue, and pleasure. He simply says that for a person who has amassed wealth, virtue and pleasure can be easily obtained to complete his life.

Every maxim in a chapter conveys a unique idea, and all the maxims put together constitute a whole. No conclusion can be drawn by a reader who ignores eight maxims in a chapter. We have shown earlier how the other maxims in a chapter complement the idea expressed by a particular maxim. In this chapter, we focused on maxim 760. Valluvar's message is that a person's wealth can pave the way to a virtuous and joyful life. But how would the poet like the wealth to be acquired? He answers this in maxim 754:

அறன்ஈனும் இன்பமும் ஈனும் திறனறிந்து
தீதின்றி வந்த பொருள் (754)

> Blameless wealth acquired by the fairest means
>
> Brings virtue and also bliss.

Wealth can be used as a tool to practice charity and experience joy. Valluvar qualifies "wealth acquired by fair, honest, and harmless means" in maxim 754. The poet wants the seeker of wealth to tread the righteous path, so that no harm is caused to anyone. Wealth acquired by such means yields virtue and joy. He has emphasized the need to acquire wealth earlier and also recognizes that it can facilitate a good life. Some people may have a single-minded desire to acquire wealth without bothering about the legality and morality of the means used to acquire it. Valluvar declares unequivocally that only wealth acquired by fair, acceptable means yields a life of virtue and joy. The maxim characterizes the wealth acquired by such means as blemish-less wealth.

Valluvar packs many words and ideas into this short poem. He wants us to learn the skills (திறனறிந்து) of wealth acquisition. The means used should not cause any harm (தீதின்றி); wealth acquired in such a fashion yields virtue and joy. Thus, the poet does not exalt the acquisition of wealth by dubious methods. People acquiring wealth by deceit, perfidy, murder, and other unethical means will bring shame on themselves, and they will be unable to experience true joy. Again, note that Valluvar refers to joy (இன்பம்) as any experience that brings happiness; there is no specific reference to sex. It is therefore inexplicable that Nagaswamy finds his "matching source" in an adult manual!

Valluvar interconnects the triad – virtue, wealth, and joy – at the end of the chapter in his final maxim (maxim 760), which we have seen earlier. Before this final maxim, he touches on the relationship between virtue and wealth. Love is one of the virtues that ranks high for Valluvar. Love expresses itself as grace in many forms: care, acceptance, tolerance, kindness, forgiveness, gratitude, etc. In maxim 757, Valluvar says that grace is the offspring of love, nourished by a foster mother called wealth:

அருளென்னும் அன்பீன் குழவி பொருளென்னும்
செல்வச் செவிலியால் உண்டு (757)

> Grace, the child of Love, is nourished
> by a foster mother called Wealth.

Love is the mother of grace. A loving citizen will be able to exhibit grace and be moved by suffering and hunger. The love within him will make him empathize with a hungry child; he may even become a little agitated by the sight. He may think of helping the child. However, a gentle graceful heart alone cannot feed the hungry. Valluvar brings in a foster mother, Wealth (means), which ensures the child will be fed well. Even a king or government with the best intentions cannot feed the people without earning revenue.

In conclusion, we can see how Valluvar connects the pieces of the wealth acquisition puzzle in intricate detail. While presenting his idealized view of wealth acquisition, he delineates the interplay and interconnections that keep the wealth wheel turning. He systematically shows why wealth is needed to sustain grace and joy. A simple Sanskrit Sutra that ranks wealth, virtue, and sex in order of importance does not even begin to approach the profundity of

Valluvar's ideas in this chapter. With this, we bring down the curtains on yet another abject failure of Nagaswamy's thesis that Thirukkural is an abridgment of the Sastras.

Chapter 13

The Life of a Householder on the Path of Aram

Nagaswamy starts with the thesis that Thirukkural is derived from the Hindu Vedic tradition. Then he clumsily tries to fit some of Valluvar's maxims to Manusmriti, the Bhagavad Gita, Ramayana, and other Sanskrit texts. Typically, he takes a maxim from a particular chapter in Thirukkural and compares it with a Sanskrit work whose context is different. Sometimes, he does not find a parallel but twists the maxim in Thirukkural as he pleases. Even a high school student of Tamil can call out this chicanery.

However, the author's audience does not know Tamil and may be taken in by this subterfuge. We wish to expose this lack of scholarly integrity on the part of Nagaswamy. Also, a universal work like Thirukkural by definition cannot be bound to a narrow religious tradition.

Valluvar considers the family to be the integral unit of society. The householder is vested with the greatest responsibility, and his virtue will keep society on the righteous path. The chapter on the life of a householder clearly sets the stage for the larger part of the ideals discussed in the book.

There is clarity and coherence in every chapter. We can interpret a maxim as we please when we read it on its own, but we will then fail to connect this maxim with the other maxims in the chapter. Nagaswamy uses only three out of ten maxims in the chapter on the life of a householder to "establish" his thesis that Thirukkural is derived from the Vedic tradition.

Let us look at each one of them:

துறந்தார்க்கும் துவ்வா தவர்க்கும் இறந்தார்க்கும்
இல்வாழ்வான் என்பான் துணை (42)

The householder is the patron of those who have left their homes, the needy, and the aged.

Here, Valluvar states that the householder aids (supports) three kinds of people: (1) Ascetics who have abjured all the material pleasures, (2) poor people who do not have food to eat, and (3) old people who have outlived their support system.

For Nagaswamy, the three are (1) Rishis (sages), (2) Devas, and (3) Pitrus. According to Nagaswamy, the householder seeks them out and pleases them by ritually offering food and water. He then concludes that Valluvar had these rituals in mind and that it is incorrect on the part of scholars to leave out the Vedic rituals of tarpana and yajna.

The life of a householder revolves around his (1) wife, (2) children, and (3) parents. Valluvar places the responsibility of supporting all three on the householder, who would be following the right path by doing so (41):

இல்வாழ்வான் என்பான் இயல்புடைய மூவர்க்கும்
நல்லாற்றின் நின்ற துணை (41)

The one at home steadfastly supports his parents, wife, and children.

Nagaswamy does not provide an equivalent. However, he quotes 3.76 from Manusmriti, which does not seem relevant to the topic:

> **An oblation duly thrown into the fire reaches the sun, from the sun proceeds rain, from rain food, and from food, the creatures (3.76).**

Nagaswamy insists that the three are (1) bachelors, (2) forest dwellers, and (3) ascetics. He claims that the householder will give them food and thus meet the other needs of these three. He concludes with a bang – an unfounded bang, but nevertheless a bang:

> **"We may say Valluvar's Tirukural is one text that made the northern Vedic life, the most commonly accepted and followed all**

over Tamil Nadu, as it was accessible to all in their own language." He goes on to add:

"Valluvar was the unparalleled integrator of this country 2000 years ago, but it is a pity that his role has not been properly focused [sic]."

The third maxim in the chapter that Nagaswamy used for his thesis is the following:

தென்புலத்தார் தெய்வம் விருந்தொக்கல்
                  தானென்றாங்கு
ஐம்புலத்தாறு ஓம்பல் தலை (43)

The ancestors, heroes (dead), guests, kindred, self (dignity), in due degree,
these five to cherish well is charity.

Valluvar conveys the idea that the following five (*Aimpulaththaar*) are the patrons of a householder: (1)

Ancestors, (2) Heroes that are dead, (3) Guests, (4) Neighbors and relatives, and (5) Self.

There is no equivalent of this maxim in the Sanskrit Sastras, but Nagaswamy is not one to be discouraged by such a trifling detail: he says that this maxim reflects typical Hindu religious sentiment. Tamils and many South Indians worshipped brave warriors who saved tribes. Valluvar has a separate chapter on practicing hospitality toward guests. The supporting material that Nagaswamy provides for his arguments deals with ritual recital of the Vedas and *ithihasas*, a symbolic offering of food and water in the name of the rishis. He further argues that Valluvar wanted society to give respect to rishis and pitrus.

On the contrary, the Tamil people had their own heroes called *theyvams* (*theyyams*). Many South Indian tribes still worship various theyvams, who have no connection to Vedic rishis and pitrus. Theyvams were people with rare qualities who served as guides to humanity. Theyvams were revered and remembered for their heroism, valor, and strength, which enabled them to save humanity from enemies, cruelty, and hunger. They are regarded as divine

protectors. Some of these theyvams became known for their kindness and love, noble character and behavior, integrity, and chastity, and served as exemplars of virtue. They were known as divines of their clans. It has become a tradition to revere and worship them as great saviors and guides by raising memorials to honor their memory (Narayanasamy 2008). Ordinary people did not recite the Vedas, because Dharmasastra prohibited their recital by common folk.

Nagaswamy avoids the subject of how guests are to be treated according to Manusmriti. We shall discuss this to establish that the life of the householder as envisaged by Valluvar is different from that described in Dharmasastra.

> **The Vaishya and the Sudra also, when arriving as guests, the host should feed, along with his servants – showing his compassionate disposition (3.112)**

He should offer a seat, room, bed, following, and attendance of the best kind to superiors, of the inferior kind to inferiors, and of the equal (ordinary) kind to equals (3.107)

He who, having eaten at a śrāddha, gives the leavings to a śūdra – this foolish man falls headlong into the Kālasūtra hell (3.249)

Manu prescribes a graded treatment of guests based on their caste and status. Valluvar has unequivocally conferred equality via birth (972) on all humans. Thirukkural also asserts that status and position do not confer greatness; it is noble thoughts and deeds that confer greatness. Persons in high positions who have a mean mentality cannot be placed on a pedestal because of their high rank in society, and noble men in lower positions cannot be despised (973):

மேலிருந்தும் மேலல்லார் மேலல்லர் கீழிருந்தும்
கீழல்லார் கீழல் லவர் (973)

> An eminent person who commits base acts is not
> great,
> nor is a lowly placed person who does noble
> deeds, base.

In conclusion, chapter 5 in Thirukkural, which deals with family life, has ten maxims. For Thirukkural to be an abridgment of the Vedic Hindu Sastras, the ideas contained in the two texts must match. Nagaswamy has analyzed only three maxims, but he cannot come up with even one sastra that has the same ideas as those expressed by Valluvar. Both the Sastras and Thirukkural agree that ancestors should be revered, but Thirukkural does not advocate symbolic rituals and offerings. Valluvar wants the householder to be the pillar of support for his neighbors, relatives, guests, the poor and weak, and old people who have outlived their children. He also wants the householder to honor his dead ancestors and heroes.

Chapter 14

Humility and Self-Restraint: The Passports to Immortality

In today's competitive world, humility is a great tool that enables us to see ourselves as we are. We view ourselves as neither superior nor inferior to anyone. We regard humility as a self-improvement tool to help us realize our own self-worth and dignity. We do not see others as having less value or being less important. Leaders appreciate the strengths of their team members and assign duties to them in order to help them achieve the best team performance. They recognize the areas their team members need help in and provide training so that they grow. Humility is thus a necessary tool to lead a successful team or company.

Valluvar views humility as the passport to earning everlasting fame. It is well understood that in this life on Earth, nobody lives forever. We all die, but a few earn everlasting fame through their conduct and deeds. They are remembered even after their death and are referred to as Amarar. Valluvar reckons that humility and self-restraint are the qualities that can place a person on the high pedestal of Amarar (Immortals).

However, lack of self-restraint can cast a pall of gloom, leading to despair. One who cannot control his senses can be easily misled, be confused about his path in life, and end up in a dark alley with ignorant fools for company.

அடக்கம் அமரருள் உய்க்கும் அடங்காமை
ஆரிருள் உய்த்து விடும் (121)

Humility earns lasting fame, grace, and wisdom;
waywardness casts gloom and darkness.

We read that humility is also a tool that helps sustain wealth, and it is also an asset to wealthy people today (Rampton 2018). In the urge for external validation, we may want to flaunt our wealth. This display often annoys others.

Because wealthy people are often public figures, their conduct toward other people becomes public knowledge.

A humble person generally can afford to be frugal and spend money where it really matters, by helping charities and noble causes. This in turn builds a person's character; she will eschew arrogance and become a positive role model.

In maxim 125, Valluvar states that humility is beneficial for everybody and is the crown jewel of a person's wealth. Anyone seeking growth in business and personal development will find this precept remarkably relevant in meeting his objectives.

எல்லார்க்கும் நன்றாம் பணிதல் அவருள்ளும்
செல்வர்க்கே செல்வம் தகைத்து (125)

Humility is good for all; to the rich it adds a

higher wealth.

Restraint of the Tongue

It is important to show restraint in our speech. One must guard against a loose tongue even if one does not guard against anything else, otherwise the repercussions could be painful. We must guard against expressions of the mind, the body, and the tongue. Among these, our tongue is the most vicious; we need to restrain and curb it. The tongue is unruly. Because it is like a very cruel weapon, Valluvar's maxim says that those who do not control it will fall into trouble and suffer.

A word from the mouth is like an arrow shot from a bow; once released, it cannot be taken back. The damage it inflicts cannot be easily undone. Words spoken arrogantly and disrespectfully to anyone can cause harm. Speaking disparagingly about a person in his absence can cause harm. Verbal offences include speaking slanderously, spreading false information about someone in his absence, creating false opinions about someone, creating enmity, backbiting, and hurtful speech. Valluvar warns about the harm caused by not restraining the tongue:

யாகாவார் ஆயினும் நாகாக்க காவாக்கால்
சோகாப்பர் சொல்லிழுக்குப் பட்டு (127)

Control of the tongue is more important than
control of anything else;

else our own words will lead us to disaster.

The Tortoise and Self-Restraint

Tortoises and turtles evoke different thoughts and feelings
in various cultures across the world. They are sturdy, live
long, move slowly, and are steadfast. Slow and peaceful,
they have been depicted in some cultures as incredibly
wise. Children in the West are told the hare and tortoise
story to learn the lesson that one who is steadfast will
succeed.

Although they are commonly known to be slow and steady,
sea turtles are very clever and travel long distances. They

are capable of utilizing the tides and moving great distances across the oceans. In African myths, they are known to be wise creatures, capable of figuring out a way out of dangerous situations.

In Tamil literary works, the tortoise is referred to in many places for its ability to shield itself from harm by using its shell. Thirumanthiram and Seevaka Chintamani talk about the ability of tortoises to shield themselves from predators (harm); likewise, humans should guard themselves from harm by restraining the five senses: touch, smell, taste, sight, and hearing. In Tamil, the five senses are commonly referred to as Aimpori (ஐம்பொறி). The ability to control the five senses gives us a protective shield like the shell of the tortoise. Notably, the tortoise also shields itself by tucking its four legs and head into its shell.

பெருமை சிறுமை அறிந்தெம் பிரான்போல்

அருமை எளிமை அறிந்தறி வாரார்

ஒருமையுள் ஆமைபோல் உள்ளைந் தடக்கி

இருமையுங் கெட்டிருந் தார்புரை அற்றே

(திருமந்திரம் 133)

Those who know glory and dishonor

Remain aware of greatness and simplicity like my

Lord

Hold the five senses within the shell like a tortoise

Free of fault are those who beat the cycle of birth

and death

ஐவகைப் பொறியும் வாட்டி,

ஆமையின் அடங்கி, ஐந்தின்

மெய்வகை தெரியுஞ் சிந்தை

விளக்கும் நின்றெரிய விட்டுப்

(Seevaka Chintamani 2834)

Hold the five senses within the shell like a tortoise

Valluvar's reference to the tortoise occurs in the chapter on self-restraint. He declares that a person who restrains his five senses will be protected, just like the tortoise that tucks its four feet and head into its shell:

ஒருமையுள் ஆமைபோல் ஐந்தடக்கல் ஆற்றின்

எழுமையும் ஏமாப் புடைத்து (126)

125

Controlling the senses like a tortoise and focusing
on results affords everlasting protection.

Valluvar's reference to the tortoise is in the larger context
of exercising self-restraint. In the chapter, Valluvar also
calls for humility, composure, refraining from uttering
words that hurt fellow human beings, and guarding against
anger.

We saw how the tortoise's ability to protect itself from harm
is often referred to. It is a familiar image that is used by
many poets. In all the above examples, we saw Kural,
Thirumanthiram, and Seevaka Chintamani focus on the
importance of restraining human senses, just as a tortoise
withdraws its four feet and head into its shell.

Nagaswamy, in his book *Thirukural: An Abridgement of
Sastras*, latches on to the tortoise to find a parallel in the
Sastras. He sets out to establish the thesis that Valluvar
borrowed from the essence of Sanskrit works to come up
with his maxims, and thus arrives at this conclusion:
"Thirukkural is a Hindu work on the art of living." His
overzealousness has led to many misinterpretations of

Thirukkural and resulted in glaring mistakes, which we have pointed out earlier.

In regard to this turtle analogy, Nagaswamy talks about the Bhagavad Gita 2.58:

> **One who is able to withdraw the senses from their objects, just as a tortoise withdraws its limbs into its shell, is established in divine wisdom. 2.58**

Valluvar emphasizes the protection offered by restraining the senses. The Bhagavad Gita offers divine wisdom. They seem similar, but they are not the same; they are different.

Further, where are the maxims in the Sastras that are parallel to the other ideas expressed in the chapter: humility, composure, utterance of the right words, and guarding against anger?

Chapter 15

Excellence of Wife and Children

Valluvar has laid down a path a householder can follow to cultivate many virtues and thus achieve greatness. He devotes a chapter to describing the fortune of having a good wife. A householder is held in high regard and considered great if his wife is blessed with an excellent disposition. Good children are jewels that adorn that goodness (60):

மங்கலம் என்ப மனைமாட்சி மற்றதன்
நன்கலம் நன்மக்கட் பேறு (60)

For a householder, an excellent wife adds luster to his crown,
and good children are his crown jewels.

Valluvar describes the greatness of a partner in a marriage. The word *mangalam* (மங்கலம்) connotes sheen, luster, and beauty. A pair of disciplined, good-natured partners that share similar lofty ideals make up an ideal household. Good children add sheen to the household. The poet describes that additional distinction of being blessed with good children. Here, the qualifier *good* (நன்) is understood from the reference to the exemplar (Sanron) elsewhere in his treatise, where he talks about the mother's joy when her child is called a Sanron (maxim 69).

The closest matching Sastras that Nagaswamy finds and quotes are from Manusmriti 9.137 and 9.138:

> **137:** Through a son, he conquers the worlds, through a son's son he obtains immortality, but through his son's grandson, he gains the world of the sun.

> **138:** Because a son delivers (*trayate*) his father from hell called Put, he was therefore called put-tra (a deliverer from Put) by the Self-existent (*Svayambhu*) himself.

Even a casual reader will understand the two verses from Manusmriti. The clear differentiation between a boy and a girl child has now become a norm in Hindu society. Having a son is somehow considered a greater achievement than having a daughter. A son is considered to somehow save the father from hell. A son confers immortality. This belief continues to this day. Manusmriti even offers a father who cannot beget a son the vicarious consolation that his daughter may one day have a son!

According to Manusmriti, there is no difference in this world between the son of a son and the son of a daughter, for even the son of a daughter saves the son-less person in the next world, like the son of a son (9.139).

Valluvar's maxim is about the excellence of a wife and child; there is not a hint of gender discrimination in the maxim. Nagaswamy, a learned Padma-Bhushan-awarded author, knows very well that the Sastras from Manusmriti have nothing in common with Valluvar's maxim (maxim 60), and Nagaswamy's followers will understand this if they read page 186 of his book. The discussion there also exposes the prejudice against daughters that is inherent in our Hindu societal beliefs.

Chapter 16

How to Use Word Power Successfully

Thirukkural is a weaving together of chapters on topics related to many aspects of leading a successful life. It is a work on the art of living. The beauty of Valluvar's maxims lies in their relevance to even modern life. The poet has arranged his work into chapters with ten maxims per chapter to cover the core ideas of a topic. One of the salient and distinct aspects of his work is that it addresses not just the king or ruler alone. The author also reaches out to the common man by providing guidelines for him. The maxims are not rules or diktats; they are guidelines that the reader is free to interpret and adapt to her life.

The chapter on the power of words applies to everyone irrespective of profession, ethnicity, and country of origin. Nagaswamy, the author of *Thirukural: An Abridgement of Sastras*, attempts to draw a parallel from Mahabharata, from which he presents a "match" for one of the ten maxims in the chapter. His claim is that Valluvar based his chapter on the power of words on the following quote from Mahabharata: "When the kingdom is threatened with an invasion, the king goes to the country and begs for war loans and benevolence by speaking out in sweet, soft and convincing style" (Mahabharata Santi-88, 26/34).

Let us put the above quote in context. It specifically applies to a king in a time of distress, to a king seeking war funds. It strains credulity when something written for this special circumstance is extrapolated to all contexts and persons. Further, Thirukkural has maxims that convey the importance of the power of words in everyday life.

Nagaswamy quotes the following maxim as being parallel to the above quote from Mahabharata:

சொல்லுக சொல்லைப் பிறிதோர்சொல்

அச்சொல்லை

வெல்லுஞ்சொல் இன்மை அறிந்து (645)

Deliver your speech after assuring yourself that no riposte can defeat it.

Valluvar in this maxim wants us to carefully select the right words to express our ideas. If we are in a hurry, we will fumble and flounder, wasting words. The goal of choosing words carefully is to get the message across to the audience or the reader as effectively as possible. He does not want us to regret hastily chosen words. Valluvar reckons that carefully chosen words are "words that bring victory and success" (வெல்லும்சொல்). He wants us to choose the best words that effectively communicate our ideas.

Here, Valluvar talks about deploying words to convey ideas. Many words can express the same idea. Among these, the words that best communicate our message to the audience have to be chosen. We can choose words that are rich in meaning and effect, yet clearly define the message we want to convey. The poet wants us to check that we have not overlooked other words that have the same – or a more powerful – effect. That is the level of effort the poet expects us to put into the preparation of a speech or write-up.

Maxim 645 applies to anyone delivering a speech in front of an audience. It talks about the thought and preparation that must go into a speech. It applies to anybody, not just a king; and to any circumstance, not just to collect war funds. The idea that Valluvar conveys is applicable today to the common man, a lawyer delivering a judgment, a manager giving his team a pep talk, or a student defending his research thesis.

He teaches the reader the power of words in this chapter and implicitly draws connections to various other maxims in other chapters. Valluvar wants the public speaker to be aware of the capacity of the audience (*திறனறிந்து*) and choose appropriate and useful words. The emphasis on "conformity with the immediate world" is referred to here. He deems it a virtue that will benefit the speaker.

திறனறிந்து சொல்லுக சொல்லை அறனும்
பொருளும் அதனினூஉங்கு இல் (644)

Speak words adapted well to various audiences;
No higher virtue lives, no gain is more surely great.

However, one may wonder what virtue he is referring to here. We use the principle of augmentation (see the Appendix). In his first canto on virtue, Valluvar stresses an important attribute, namely, the ability to conform to our surroundings and fit into the world. He states that people who did not learn to conform with the world may have studied many books but are not knowledgeable (maxim 140):

உலகத்தோடு ஒட்ட ஒழுகல் பலகற்றும்
கல்லார் அறிவிலா தார்   (140)

Who know not with the world in harmony to dwell,
May many things have learned, but nothing well.

Audience analysis is a topic now in schools that teach communication. Successful leaders today cannot go to a memorial of a beloved community member and speak about any topic they choose. The audience expects to hear about the honorable deeds of the departed person. Even technical leaders can lose their audience by not calibrating their talk to the capacity of the listener. One cannot explain the details of genetic engineering to new college students who do not have a foundation in genetics.

Valluvar's work itself is a testament to the power of words. The poet picked the shortest grammatical meter in Tamil poetry to compose his work. He packed information in an orderly, economical, and powerful way to convey messages on many aspects of the art of living. Maxim 649 is about economy in word choice when addressing a gathering. For example, take the historical Gettysburg address of President Lincoln. He used less than 275 words after the main speaker had spoken for two hours. He addressed the nation after the brutal civil war, and the location was in the place where the dead were laid to rest. He was there to consecrate the dead soldiers. This speech has become a milestone in history.

பலசொல்லக் காமுறுவர் மன்றமாசு அற்ற

சிலசொல்லல் தேற்றா தவர் (649)

They over-speak who do not seek

Few, clear, and flawless words to speak.

The president was preceded by Edward Everett, who had spoken for two hours. Everett reflected on Lincoln's speech and wrote to him, "I wish that I could flatter myself that I had come as near to the central idea of the occasion in two hours as you did in two minutes." Great men know the power of words and use it to fit the occasion and audience. The civil war was over, but the question of slavery was not yet settled in the country. The president's speech reminded the audience of 15,000 about the nation's obligation to uphold the principles and vision of the founding fathers that "all men were created equal." The flawless clarity and economy of words mentioned in maxim 649 are reflected in Lincoln's famous speech.

Nagaswamy is not able to come up with a single idea from the Sastras that matches the maxims in the chapter on the power of words. He quotes a Sastra and baldly tells the reader that it is parallel to Valluvar's chapter on the power of words. Any serious student of Valluvar and Tamil will easily see through Nagaswamy's vacuous assertions.

Each maxim in a chapter conveys a unique idea on the subject. To justify his thesis that Thirukkural is indeed an abridgment of the Sastras, Nagaswamy will have to find truly parallel ideas that cover the complete set of maxims in a chapter. He has skipped many gems in this chapter of Thirukkural, evidently because he has failed to find parallels for them in the Sastras.

Chapter 17

Nagaswamy's Other Acts of Commission and Omission

Nonexistent Sources

Manjai Vasanthan has pointed out one instance of a nonexistent source. In the following example, we find that the Sanskrit equivalent Nagaswamy quoted on page 126 of his book is not even present in the literature. Thirukkural asserts that the one virtue that supersedes all the other virtues we can possess is a spotless mind devoid of faults and vices. The rest of the external show we put on is mere noise.

> மனத்துக்கண் மாசிலன் ஆதல் அனைத்தறன்
> ஆகுல நீர பிற (34)

Right action is purity of heart and mind – all else is hollow sounds.

Nagaswamy says that he "found" a matching verse for this maxim in the Bhagwad Gita 3.78. He goes on to explain: "Gita has the following: Fearlessness, spotless purity, stability of knowledge and yoga, gift, peace of mind, sacrifice and learning constitute real tapas."

Unfortunately for him, chapter 3 of the Bhagwad Gita (Karma Yoga) has only 43 verses. The matching verse does not even exist, and even the explanation he gives does not represent the true meaning of Kural's maxim. Valluvar's maxim stresses that "intent" and "purity of mind" are more important than the extravagant shows and rituals we perform.

Confusing Charity with Hospitality

Charity (ஈகை) is voluntary aid rendered to those in need, from humanitarian motives. Valluvar wants the householder to serve the destitute, that is, people who cannot meet the basic necessities of food, shelter, and clothing.

He says that wealth used to wipe out the intense hunger of the destitute is not expended; rather, it is a safe investment (226).

Valluvar says:

அற்றார் அழிபசி தீர்த்தல் அஃதொருவன்
பெற்றான் பொருள்வைப் புழி (226)

Ending the ruinous hunger of the poor – a safe that stores a person's wealth.

The Tamil poet Avvaiyar describes hunger as driving away ten valued human qualities; honor, respect, education, caring, wisdom, giving, penance, high status, effort, and even sexuality. Valluvar would rather have us put our money where it belongs. He considers the money and effort spent on removing hunger a safe investment.

மானம் குலம்கல்வி வண்மை அறிவுடைமை
தானம் தவம்உயர்ச்சி தாளாண்மை-தேனின்
கசிவந்த சொல்லியர்மேல் காமுறுதல் பத்தும்
பசிவந் திடப்பறந்து போம்

Respect, honor, education, caring

wisdom, high status, effort, giving,

pennace - even love for sweet voice of maidens -

all ten disappear as hunger strikes hard

The parallel that Nagaswamy quotes from Manusmriti is as follows:

IIe himself should not eat what he does not offer to his guest. The honoring of guests is conducive to wealth, fame, longevity, and heaven (3.106)

This Sastra conveys how a householder should display his hospitality. A guest is not the destitute (அற்றார்) that Valluvar is talking about. Valluvar has covered hospitality (விருந்தோம்பல்) separately. IIe devotes a chapter to charity (chapter 22) and another to hospitality (chapter 8). We ask again: Where is the evidence for Nagaswamy's claim that Thirukkural is an abridgment of the Sastras?

Desperately Bridging Disparate Verses

Valluvar's Thirukkural is unique in content and style. Some of the ideas in it may exist in other places. However, the conclusion that the whole work is an abridgment of the Sastras does not hold water, because the supporting evidence does not exist – except in Nagaswamy's imagination. This effort smacks of desperation in the scholastic domain. Nagaswamy cherry-picks a few couplets of Valluvar and tries to identify matching slokas from Sanskrit sources. He desperately tries to show that the couplets express the same sentiments as the slokas. But when we read the kural in Tamil, look at the commentary, and compare it with his Sanskrit sources, the falsity of his claim becomes transparent. We show another example from page 126 of his book: Nagaswamy takes maxim 41 on domestic life and cites Manusmriti 3.56 as a similar "idea" from the other side.

இல்வாழ்வான் என்பான் இயல்புடைய மூவர்க்கும்
நல்லாற்றின் நின்ற துணை (41)

Family life is the best protection for

one's parents, spouse, and children.

The Tamil original talks about the virtue of a householder. In maxim 42, Valluvar asserts that the householder alone supports the other three social classes, who in his commentaries are 1) people who have left for the forests but are still married, 2) bachelors, and 3) ascetics. These three classes are able to carry out their duties well only because others live as good householders, working ceaselessly for those who have renounced work along with the world and all other aspects of life.

Nagaswamy quotes the following from Manusmriti (3:56) as being remarkably similar:

Where women are honored, there the gods

rejoice; where, on the other hand, they are

not honored, there all rites are fruitless

(3.56)

We see no emphasis on family life in the above.

Thiruvalluvar gives pride of place to family life. He is the first great philosopher and poet to do so, at a time when renunciation was the only acceptable path to greatness and to salvation. In Valluvar's synthesis of matter and spirit, and of life affirmation and life negation, domestic life is the most desirable way of life, provided it is practiced along the path of "Aram" (Schweitzer 2013).

In the larger sphere, Aram, the virtuous path described by Valluvar, falls into two divisions: one is Family Life (இல்லறம்) and the second is Ascetic Life (துறவறம்). Although family life was the more popular path, a few took to renunciation for salvation in those days. Ascetics, who had renounced the world, needed support from householders. Valluvar makes the family unit and the householder responsible for hosting and feeding ascetics. He regards family life and the householder as superior to the ascetic way of life and the ascetic, respectively.

Valluvar declares that the householder who lives in the right way is superior to the ascetic who aspires for a better life in the next world:

ஆற்றின் ஒழுக்கி அறனிழுக்கா இல்வாழ்க்கை
நோற்பாரின் நோன்மை உடைத்து (48)

The path of righteousness in family life is saintlier
than the saint's path.

He even says that those who have stayed true to all the
righteous ideals of family life – practicing love, charity,
truth, and keeping anger, jealousy, and all vices at bay – are
raised in fame alongside celestial beings:

வையத்துள் வாழ்வாங்கு வாழ்பவன் வான்உறையும்
தெய்வத்துள் வைக்கப் படும் (50)

He is a man of divine worth
Who lives in an ideal home on Earth.

Thus, the core emphasis and exaltation of the householder's
way of life after laying out its virtues unambiguously
distinguishes Valluvar's teachings from the Sastras.
Nagaswamy has not touched on the above aspects of

Thirukkural, evidently because he has failed to find matching material in the Sastras. His abridgement thesis is therefore an exercise in futility.

The Missing Canto

Nagaswamy has not even attempted to find a match in the Sastras for 25 chapters (out of the 133 chapters in Thirukkural) that deal with Eros. We quote from a well-known Indologist, Kamil Zvelebil:

Thiruvalluvar's "Eros" is utterly different from any of the Sanskrit Kama sastras. While Vatsyayana's work (and all later Sanskrit erotology) is Sastra, that is, objective and scientific analysis of sex, the third part of the Kural is a poetic picture of eros, of ideal love, of its dramatic situations. As a work of literary art, [it] reveals a single structural plan, and looks like a work of a single master. In the erotic couplets of the third part (Kamaththuppaal), the teacher, the preacher in Valluvar has stepped aside, and the poet speaks almost the language of the superb love poetry of the Classical Age. (Kamil Zvelebil)

Conclusions

Thirukkural is a comprehensive work covering many topics on the art of living: domestic virtues, an abhorrence of taking life, not surrendering to anger, curbing greed, administration, war, rain, friendship, truthfulness, enemies, administration, country, renunciation, love, and more. Nagaswamy's thesis that Thirukkural is an abridgment of Sastras is patently unfounded. First, the author has not even picked a sufficient number of couplets from Thirukkural to analyze; 100 or so couplets from a total of 1,330 is too small a sample to support his thesis. His sampling of Thirukkural is thus grossly inadequate. Each maxim in Thirukkural has a unique idea. We have shown that even in the samples Nagaswamy has studied, he has not interpreted the kurals correctly. In order to find evidence from Thirukkural that matches the idea explicitly conveyed in the Sanskrit Sastras, Nagaswamy even misrepresents the original sources; in one instance, the originally quoted source does not even exist. This points to a clear lack of academic integrity. A careful reading of his work exposes many abuses of scholarship, such as mixing up ideas and misrepresenting related ideas as being identical. For example, charity is different from hospitality, and Valluvar treats them in separate chapters. Nagaswamy also spins conclusions out of thin air without supporting evidence. His idea seems to be that if a lie is repeated enough times, readers will believe it. Some of the lapses are so flagrant that no institution of repute will accept the work even for a master's level dissertation. The book itself is poorly written but has become talked about, as attested to by the publicity, the Padma Bhushan award, and even the recognition lavished on the author. Those who know contemporary India will have no difficulty in identifying the ideological wellsprings of support for Nagaswamy's book; they are hiding in plain sight.

Appendix: Coupling of Kurals

Complementation

Thirukkural is a multi-layered work that deals with many ideals. The maxims can be studied on their own as individual couplets. The ten maxims in a chapter complement each other. Neglecting the complementation effect and analyzing the maxims individually will not do justice to the masterpiece. For example, maxim 291 defines truthfulness (*vaaymai*):

வாய்மை எனப்படுவது யாதெனின்
யாதொன்றும்
தீமை இலாத சொலல் (291)

What is truthfulness? It is nothing
but utterance that causes no harm.

Truth is speaking words that do not inflict the least harm on others. There may be situations where speaking the truth may harm others. Sometimes, a lie can save a good person from harm. Valluvar answers this in his next couplet:

பொய்மையும் வாய்மை யிடத்த புரைதீர்ந்த

நன்மை பயக்கும் எனின் (292)

Even falsehood has the character of truth,

if it bestows benefit devoid of vice.

Even falsehood partakes of the nature of truth if it confers a benefit that is free from fault; i.e., if it does not involve inflicting harm on others.

My high school Tamil teacher, Pulavar Sundaramurthi, used to explain this passionately. When we are given a certain finite number of maxims to commit to memory, the other maxims are neglected, leading to an incomplete picture of the whole piece.

Valluvar mentions that greatness is not achieved by birth as all of us are born in the same way from our mothers (*பிறப்பொக்கும் எல்லா வுயிர்க்கும்* – 972). One of the maxims in a chapter can be interpreted in a particular way, but the author's intent becomes clear when we read all the maxims in the chapter. This is why a well-informed commentator connects and cross-references the maxims to support his point.

Hierarchies have been assigned and greatness attributed to some people based on their birth-based caste. Valluvar lived when these hierarchies were already set. His first maxim in chapter 98 dismantles this differential greatness and status due to birth by treating birth as the great equalizer (பிறப்பொக்கும் எல்லா வுயிர்க்கும் – 972). We are all born by the same process. Nobody is born from the mouth of Brahma, for example, and therefore deserves a special place; we are all born through the same process from the womb of our mothers.

But somehow a hierarchical system was established. Even in such an environment, he goes on to assert that "one's higher place in the social strata – due to caste, economics, legacy, lineage – does not automatically translate to greatness." Greatness is not earned by being placed up there (மேலிருந்தும் மேலல்லார் மேல்லல்லர் – 973).

Why does Valluvar say this?

மேலிருந்தும் மேலல்லார் மேலல்லர்

கீழிருந்துங்

கீழல்லார் கீழல் லவர் (973)

Ignoble and high, not great they are,
The noble low, not low they are.

A person may be placed low down in the hierarchy by caste, lineage, economics, and so on. But if his conduct is flawless and he has rare achievements to his credit, then he is not down there (கீழிருந்தும் கீழல்லார் கீழல்லவர்).

A good commentator teaches us how to read Thirukkural properly or at least explains how she arrived at her notes. She walks us through the complementation process we describe here. A maxim – for example, maxim 972 – in Thirukkural is great on its own. But it becomes more meaningful when it is complemented by other maxims, for example, maxim 973, in the same chapter.

Augmentation

Augmentation is an increase in value, size, weight, or quality. Both complementation and augmentation occur when we read maxims in their entirety and connect them, making it a holistic experience. Thirukkural is weaved in that fashion; the work is not a bunch of stand-alone maxims.

When we study the chapter on learning (kalvi-கல்வி), chapter 39, we need to connect the effect and benefit of learning – gaining knowledge (அறிவுடைமை- aRivudaimai) – with chapter 42. This cross-connection will augment our understanding of the maxims in the learning chapter.

Valluvar authored many theses before we had universities and degrees. In any area of research, we need to cite and reference. Nobody can recall every related work in a space-limited thesis or research essay. It is customary practice to cite supporting documents in our work. The references help the reader in many ways; for example, they give the reader the contextual framework relative to the objective and results of the article; the reader will also understand how we deviated from and improved on earlier work.

We saw how Valluvar supports his maxims within the chapter by complementation.

Every single maxim can be studied in isolation too, but that would not convey the whole story. A maxim is just a brick or column of the room the author has built for us. He has thought about the edifice and broken it down into smaller structures for us to digest one by one; the whole edifice is made up of individual maxims, and we need to piece them together to get the full picture.

After reading the maxims in a chapter, one may feel satisfied that all the pieces of the puzzle have fallen in place. Our author did not give a user guide to explain how the maxims work together; he has left that work for the willing reader. Respected commentators of Thirukkural such as Paavanar teach us the art of augmentation: other chapters of Valluvar's masterpiece augment the ideas conveyed in a chapter. A keen reader will start seeing missing parts of the puzzle in other chapters and bring them to the table to strengthen her understanding of any chapter.

If I have been able to get my message across in the earlier paragraphs, I have communicated the idea of augmentation in Thirukkural reading. In the following paragraphs, I shall illustrate this idea with an example. I leave the reader to find out more by exploring Thirukkural. We have used the ideas of complementation and augmentation in this book.

Social hierarchies based on wealth, profession, and caste were well entrenched during Valluvar's time. In his chapter on greatness, he talks about equality of birth (பிறப்பொக்கும் எல்லா வுயிர்க்கும் – 972), and also states that a high place in society does not necessarily confer greatness (மேலிருந்தும் மேலல்லர் – 973).

Now, one can still ask, "Did Valluvar confront Manu's caste-based hierarchy? Did he not confront Brahmanism?" One may argue either way. One could respond, "Oh! No, there was no caste system in place; everything was based on character or profession." But there is a sting in the tail in maxim 134:

மறப்பினு மோத்துக் கொள லாகும்

பார்ப்பான்

பிறப்பொழுக்கங் குன்றக் கெடும் (134)

A Brahmin can recall forgotten lore,

But conduct lost returns no more.

A Brahmin may forget his Vedas (ஓத்து), but he can always read them again, memorize them again, and recite them. Thus, nothing is lost by forgetting the scripture. But if the Brahmin's character is flawed, he is beyond redemption. Caste determined the status of a person in his time, yet Valluvar maintained that character and conduct supersede caste and are the true benchmarks of greatness.

We may read a chapter and sometimes feel that Valluvar has given conclusive views and answered all questions on the subject within the chapter. However, we may sometimes find that through a hypertext-like link, he has answered some counterpoints elsewhere. One such example is the subject of the powerful forces of nature unleashed by the environment (ஊழ் – uuzh), which can play a significant role in determining life's outcomes. He describes some of the effects of these forces of nature in chapter 38. One may think that the poet is favoring the forces of destiny that may determine how our lives pan out; we may have to resign ourselves to our fate. But he gives an answer full of positivity and hope later, in chapter 62.

Our destiny is shaped by nature, our surroundings, the way we are raised, and genetics. We have also inherited some of our traits from our parents and ancestors. We are all wired in unique ways; we cannot be completely immune to these powerful forces. Some of these forces can serve as a source of strength as well. The effects of these forces show up in many forms depending on our surroundings and on the opportunities presented to us. However, we can do our best to overcome some or even many of these forces with determination and hard work.

Valluvar calls all these powerful forces shaping our destiny uuzh (ஊழ்). He acknowledges the power of these natural forces, many of which can oppose us in some way or another. We can read the finest of texts and gather knowledge, but it is our robust innate wisdom that will prevail (373) [*நுண்ணிய நூல் பல கற்பினும்*].

Valluvar acknowledges that these aforementioned forces of nature are omnipotent and immensely powerful (380). Nature's omnipotence has its own moods and trumps everything else. These forces of nature can supersede any other countervailing force that we can bring into play: our effort, training, and steely determination.

ஊழிற் பெருவலி யாவுள மற்றுஒன்று

சூழினும் தான்முந் துறும் (380)

Generally, natural forces are very powerful
superseding any countervailing force that
we can summon.

We can pull together many other factors (மற்று ஒன்று): training, hard work, determination, planning, and other resources at our disposal. These are factors within our control.

Can we somehow prevail? Can we defeat these powerful (பெருவலி) forces that are a part and parcel of nature? Does Valluvar ask us to submit ourselves to these powers, resign ourselves to our fate, and give up?

The poet has answered this question in maxim 620:

ஊழையும் உப்பக்கம் காண்பர்

உலைவின்றித்

தாழாது உஞற்று பவர் (620)

Ceaseless efforts without getting
overwhelmed
can deflect even natural forces.

Tireless and relentless determination (உலைவின்றி), persistence and perseverance (தாழாது), can deflect (உப்பக்கம்) even powerful natural forces.

Thus, the challenge posed by the forces of nature described in chapter 38 is met head on in chapter 62, which talks about unstinting effort. Chapter 38 is the last chapter in the virtue canto of the book, and chapter 62 discusses wealth and related material.

With this example of how we can use augmentation to improve our understanding of the intricacies of Thirukkural, we reach the end of this book. Valluvar has left many Easter eggs for us to discover in his work, which makes the study of Thirukkural a voyage without end.

References

Desigar, S. Dandapani. 1983. திருக்குறள் உரைச்சளஞ்சியம் (in Tamil) [Thirukkural Commentary]. Madurai: Madurai Kamarajar University.

Devaneyan, N., 1969. திருக்குறள் தமிழ் மரபுரை (in Tamil) [Thirukkural Commentary] Chennai: Pari Press.

Ilaiah, Kancha. 2021. "The Shudra Kings and Brahmins: A Mirror Image of History." *Mainstream Weekly,* September 3. https://www.mainstreamweekly.net/article11498.html.

Jensen, Derrick. 2006. "Responsibility (p. 176)". From Chapter Titled "Abuse." In *Endgame, Volume 1: The Problem of Civilization.* Vol. 1. New York: Seven Stories Press. https://derrickjensen.org/endgame/responsibility/.

Jha, G. 1920. *Manusmrithi with Commentary of Medhatithi.* Calcutta: University of Calcutta.

Maharasan, E. 2021. வேளாண் மரபின் தமிழ் அடையாளம் (in Tamil) [Tamil identity in Agricultural Heritage]. Chennai: Yappu Publications.

Narayanasamy, J. 2008. *Thirukural: Transliteration and Translation.* Chennai: Sura Publications.

Nagaswamy, R. 2017. *Thirukural: An Abridgement of Sastras.* Giri Trading Agency Private Limited.

Nedunchezhiyan, "Navalar" R. 1991. *Thirukkural: Aratthuppaal* (in Tamil) [Thirukkural Notes and Commentary]. Chennai: Uma Padhippagam.

Pope, G.U. 1886. *Thirukural, English Translation and Commentary.* London: W.H. Allen & Co.

Prabhakaran, R. 2020. *The Ageless Wisdom: As Embodied in Thirukkural.* Kindle. Chennai: Emerald Publishers.

Prabhupada, A.C. 1972. *Shrimad Bhagavatam.* New York: Bhakthi Vedanta Book Trust.

Pruiksma, T.H. 2021. *The Kural, Translated from Tamil.* Boston: Beacon Press.

Rampton, John. 2018. "10 Brutal Lessons You Need to Learn Before Getting Rich." *Entrepreneur.* https://www.entrepreneur.com/living/10-brutal-lessons-you-need-to-learn-before-getting-rich/309812.

Rodriguez, Andrea. 2014. "Cuba Looks to Mangroves to Fend off Rising Seas." *PHYS.ORG.* https://phys.org/news/2014-07-cuba-mangroves-fend-seas.html.

Sawant, P.B. 2020. "The Manusmriti and a Divided Nation." *The Wire*, November 16. https://thewire.in/caste/manusmriti-history-discrimination-constitution.

Schweitzer, Albert 2013. Indian Thoughts and Its Development. Vancouver, British Columbia, Canada: Read Books. pp. 200–205. ISBN 978-14-7338-900-7.

Smith, J.W. 2020. "Tacit Thirukkural: Religion, Ethics, and
Poetics in a Tamil Literary Tradition." Harvard
University, Ph D Dissertation.

Swamy, V.C. Kulandai. 1994. *The Immortal Kural.* Delhi:
South Asia Books.

Tandon, T. 2020. "Ancient Indian Education System."
Jagran Josh. www.jagranjosh.com.

Vasanthan, M. 2019. *திருக்குறள்: சாத்திரங்களின் சாரமா?* (in
Tamil) [Is Thirukkural an Abridgment of the Sastras?]
Dravidar Iyakka Publishers.
https://periyarbooks.com/products/thirukkural-
sasththirangalin-saarama.

About the Author

Kathiravan Krishnamurthi, Ph.D., was born in Coimbatore, Tamil Nadu, India. After obtaining his BE (Hons) from NIT Tiruchirappalli (then REC Trichy), he came to Canada to earn his M.S and Ph.D. in Electronics. He has served both the communications and electronics industries in various capacities over the years. Mainly tasked with the design of new circuits and systems, his various designs have resulted in several commercial products and more than 14 patents.

He pursues his interest in Tamil by translation and transcreation. His Tamil book, *Fundamentals of Radio Communications* (அடிப்படை ரேடியோ தொடர்பாடல்), was nominated for the best technical book of 2013 by the Tamil Nadu Government. He collaborated with a team of enthusiasts to compile another Tamil book, அறிவியல் அறிவோம் (*Let Us Get to Know Science*), which focuses on teaching students day-to-day science. His third Tamil book, *Science through Stories* (கதைவிழி அறிவியல்), is slated to be published this year. His latest work, *Thirukkural: A Snapshot of the Sastras?*, is in English. This book, a refutation of Nagaswamy's polemical book *Thirukural: An*

Abridgement of Sastras and a detailed study of Thirukkural and its lessons, is based on a series of articles he wrote in many forums and is informed by his reading and understanding of the classic commentaries.

Kathiravan currently lives in Westford, Massachusetts, United States.